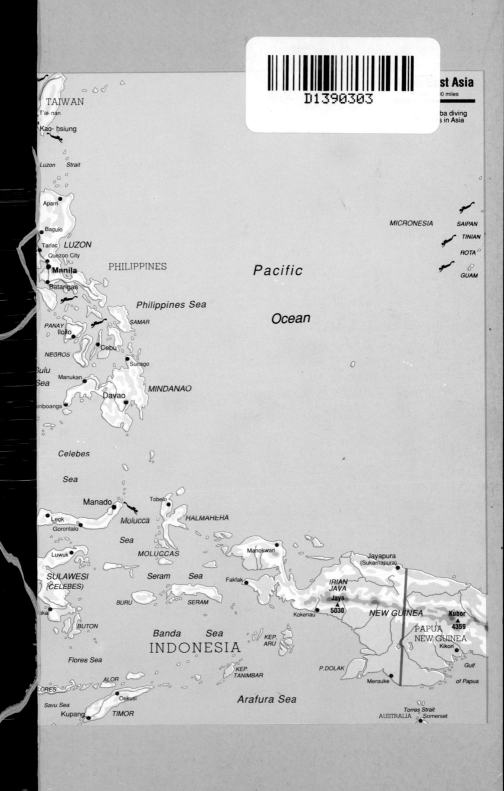

TAIWAN

T'ai-nan

Kao-hsiung

Luzon Strait

Aparri

Baguio

Tarlac LUZON

Quezon City

Manila

Batangas

PHILIPPINES

Philippines Sea

PANAY
Iloilo

SAMAR

NEGROS

Cebu

Surigao

Sulu

Manukan

Sea

Zamboanga

Davao

MINDANAO

Celebes

Sea

Manado

Tobelo

Leok

Gorontalo

Molucca
Sea

HALMAHERA

Luwuk

MOLUCCAS

Manokwari

SULAWESI
(CELEBES)

Seram Sea

Fakfak

IRIAN
JAVA

BURU

SERAM

Jaya
▲
5030

Jayapura
(Sukarnapura)

Kokenau

NEW GUINEA

Kubor
▲
4359

BUTON

Banda Sea

INDONESIA

KEP.
ARU

PAPUA
NEW GUINEA

Kikori

Flores Sea

KEP.
TANIMBAR

P.DOLAK

Gulf
of Papua

ALOR

Oekusi

Merauke

LORES

Savu Sea

Kupang TIMOR

Arafura Sea

Torres Strait

AUSTRALIA Somerset

Pacific

Ocean

MICRONESIA SAIPAN

TINIAN

ROTA

GUAM

INSIGHT GUIDES

UNDERWATER

MARINE LIFE IN THE SOUTH CHINA SEA

Written by **Margaret S. Gremli, Ph.D**
with **Helen E. Newman, M.Sc**
(Scientific Editor)
Photographs by **Singapore Club Aquanaut divers**
and others

Insight Guide Underwater:

MARINE LIFE IN THE SOUTH CHINA SEA

Directed by
Hans Höfer

Editorial Director
Geoffrey Eu

Design Concept by
V. Barl

Design by
Viscom Design

© 2001 APA Publications GmbH & Co. Verlag KG

First Edition 1993
First Edition (reprinted) 2001
All Rights Reserved

Printed in Singapore by
Insight Print Services (Pte) Ltd
Fax: 65-861 6438

Distributed in the United Kingdom & Ireland by
GeoCenter International Ltd
The Viables Center, Harrow Way
Basingstoke, Hampshire RG22 4BJ
ISBN: 9-62421-542-1

Worldwide distribution enquiries:
APA Publications GmbH & Co. Verlag KG
(Singapore Branch)
38 Joo Koon Road
Singapore 628990
ISBN: 9-62421-542-1

www.insightguides.com

Maggie Gremli with Helen Newman

Dear Reader

Welcome! You are invited to join us among the coral reefs of the South China Sea! The first time I encountered a living coral reef as a novice snorkeller is an experience I shall never forget. In spite of being trained as a biologist, I was unprepared for the profusion of life forms that exist in this tropical underwater paradise.

To venture underwater in a coral reef is to become immersed in a magical world. The vast quantities of species that coexist there gives one the feeling of being in a 360-degree, three-dimensional, technicolour cinema. No ecosystem on land can compete with the astonishing variety of shapes, sizes, colours and habits of the creatures that are associated with a coral reef ecosystem.

From being a neonate snorkeller venturing offshore to easily accessible reefs, I conquered my fear of deep water to become a certified SCUBA diver more than fourteen years ago. Since then, I have enjoyed underwater vistas in the South China Sea off the coasts of Malaysia, Indonesia, Thailand and the Philippines. From being an uninformed and distant "intruder", I have developed into a more intelligent and sensitive observer. Increasing my knowledge of coral reef life has brought greater satisfaction with each dive.

Initiated by the Singapore Club Aquanaut, this guide is intended for SCUBA divers and snorkellers, but it will also be useful for students of marine biology. Although it is not a comprehensive guide to all coral reef life in the South China Sea, this book will help you to gain a better understanding of ways in which organisms are related to each other, how they are adapted for their particular niche on the reef and why they behave the way they do.

For identification purposes, scientific names have been used. Initially, they may seem cumbersome to the casual reef observer, but they are important for several reasons. First, common names are

used arbitrarily from region to region, so the same common name may be used for different organisms. In addition, a single organism may be known by several different common names, so the scientific name is the only way to positively distinguish it from all other species.

Scientific names have two component parts – the genus name which is capitalised and the species name which is not. The genus name denotes the broader group (like a family) to which one or more species (siblings) belong. Species which belong to the same genus have certain common features, but they also have differences.

Sometimes, an organism cannot be positively identified unless it is removed from the water and examined in detail. Since all of the life forms featured in this book have been identified from photographs, it is not always possible to identify the exact species. In such cases, the species name is denoted simply as sp. (short for species). If the genus cannot be conclusively identified, a broader category name has been used.

Many people have contributed their efforts to this book. Not least are the photographers who generously donated their slides and without whose talents this book would not have been possible.

I am deeply grateful to **Helen Newman** who not only contributed approximately one-third of the slides for the book, but also acted as scientific editor, sharing her extensive knowledge in marine life and ecology of the region. A former curator of Sentosa Island's Coralarium and Director of Curatorial Services at Singapore's Underwater World, Helen is thoroughly conversant with tropical coral reefs and their species.

Other Singapore Club Aquanaut members **Gillian Ashworth**, **Anne Morrison** and **David Lane** offered their expertise as editor, illustrator and consultant marine biologist respectively. We hope this guide will inspire snorkellers and SCUBA divers to become more sensitive to, and appreciative of, the world we are privileged to enjoy. More importantly, our hope is to inspire readers to become more active in ensuring the preservation of coral reefs for future generations to enjoy.

Contents

Dear Reader 5
About This Region 11

The Coral Reefs 12

Corals
Builders of the Reef **20**
Hard Corals **21**
Octocorals **30**
   Alcyonarians **30**
   Gorgonians **34**

Coral Relatives
Sea Anemones **38**
Zoanthidea **42**
Hydrozoa **44**
   Fire Corals **44**
   Stinging Hydroids **46**
Jellyfish **48**

Plant Life
Algae **51**

Fish
Introduction **56**
Sharks and Rays **61**
Large Bony Reef Fish **72**
Common Reef Fish **82**
Bottom Dwellers **106**
Cave Dwellers **108**
Moray Eels **110**
Fish That School **112**

Invertebrates

Sponges (Porifera) **120**
Flatworms (Platyhelminths)................**124**
Segmented Worms (Annelids)............**126**
Crustaceans **129**
Molluscs (Soft-bodied Animals) **137**
   Gastropods **137**
   Nudibranchs **141**
   Bivalves **146**
   Cephalopods **149**
Sea Mats (Bryozoa) **153**
Spiny-Skinned Animals
(Echinoderms)....................................**154**
   Starfish **155**
   Brittlestars **160**
   Sea Urchins **162**
   Sea Cucumbers **167**
   Feather Stars...................................**170**
Sea Squirts (Tunicates)......................**173**

Reef Visitors

Reptiles **180**
Dolphins **185**

Features

Special Relationships..........................**188**
Marine Animals To Avoid **195**
The Reef's Latest Invaders **206**
Conservation **210**

Glossary **216**
Index **220**

Cave Corals and Blue Sponge
Although they look like small sea anemones, these brilliant orange cave corals or *Tubastrea* are actually a type of coral in which each coral polyp is large and its parts clearly visible.

ABOUT THIS REGION

South East Asia holds a strong appeal to tourists from all over the world. Both the curious visitor and the world traveller are attracted to the lure of its varied landscapes, the fascination of its diversity of cultures and festivals, the hospitable nature of its courteous and gracious people and the exotic aromas of its unending array of cuisines.

But another dimension, an often understated one, exists for this region. The seas that border the coastline, the bays and inlets that fringe its shores are a dimension that has often been taken for granted. They have, since their usefulness was discovered, acted as the mainstay of the people – a mode of transport, a source of food and commerce. Sometimes the seas have even become the avenue of flight to freedom and an opportunity of a new life in a new land.

The South China Sea, the largest marginal sea connecting to the Western Pacific, dominates this region. Its Chinese name is Nan Hai meaning Southern Sea. Embracing an area of 2,900 km from north to south and 966 km from east to west, its average depth is around 1,200 metres. This abundant body of water extends from the northern limit of mainland Asia and Taiwan to the southern limit of the waters separating Sumatra and Borneo. It is bounded on the west by the Gulf of Thailand and the east by the Philippine Islands.

This area is studded by reef shoal areas, islets and banks, some of which are drowned atolls. Some of these islands are home to simple fisherfolk while others are uninhabited.

The temperature is hot and tropical and greatly influenced by seasonal monsoons. These monsoons also control the sea surface currents enabling an exchange of water between the South China Sea and adjacent bodies of water. Surface temperature of the water is relatively warm ranging from 21°C to 29°C.

Shallow, clear warm waters surrounding many of the offshore islands that dot the South China Sea offer the underwater explorer a rich and profound experience baffling to the imagination. In these shallow tropical waters where food and shelter are plentiful, living things of all colours, shapes and sizes live and interrelate in living communities called coral reefs.

What are coral reefs? What kind of organisms live in them? Turn the pages of this guide to find out about this remarkable living community.

The Coral

The majority of reefs that exist in the South China Sea are fringing as opposed to atoll reefs. The original architects of these reefs are the stony corals that build layer upon layer of corallite homes atop those of their predecessors. Their enormous limestone fortresses are gradually built up as they extract calcium carbonate (limestone) from the chemicals in seawater to construct their homes. Algae and a variety of other invertebrate animals (sponges, worms, crustaceans, molluscs and echinoderms) coexist with numerous species of fish to form a living community that supersedes all other communities in terms of abundance and variety.

Corals may conveniently be divided into two major groups: the hermatypic or reef building corals and the ahermatypic or non-reef building corals. The hermatypic corals can reach massive proportions and are significant in building up the coral formations that comprise the reef. The skeletons of ahermatypic corals are not as robust as those of hermatypic corals and they usually disintegrate when the coral dies.

Hermatypic corals are not the only organisms responsible for building up the massive structure of the reef. Encrusting algae secrete calcareous substances which bind pieces of loose rock or rubble that have broken away from the main coral heads. Encrusting algae help to stabililise areas of the reef that are washed by strong waves. Calcareous algae also add to the attractive colouration of the reef. They range from bright pink to red in colour.

As long-lasting as these magnificent monuments are, coral reef communities are also quite fragile. The temperature of the water must not drop below 19°C and the direction and strength of the current must be just right to maintain a balanced food supply. Similarly, if light conditions are reduced by sediments and pollutants in the water, all forms of life on the reef will be severely affected.

Plankton is a collective term used to describe the huge quantity of drifting organisms present in seawater, all of which are subjected to the movement of currents and tides. Plankton is made up of an endless variety of life forms including microscopic plants and animals, as well as eggs and larval stages of larger organisms.

The two major types of planktonic forms are phytoplankton (plant forms) and zooplankton (animal forms). Phytoplankton are capable of manufacturing their own food by means of a chemical process called photosynthesis. Using energy from the sun together with carbon dioxide and other dissolved nutrients in seawater, they manufacture the organic carbohydrate materials needed to incorporate into and build up their body structure. As food producers, phytoplankton form the base of the food pyramid thus furnishing the necessary food for the animal plankton forms that feed on them. In turn, the zooplankton are preyed upon by other reef organisms, including corals, molluscs, small fish and crustaceans. Higher up in the food chain, successive levels of consumers prey on these animals until a number of large predators dominate the food chain.

Finally, at the base of the food chain but still performing a very important role on the reef, are the decomposers which consume dead organic matter. Thus, the balance of life on the reef exists interdependently. Once this balance is lost, the reef is in jeopardy.

Swimming Crab (*Thalamita sp.*)
Well camouflaged, this swimming crab is hardly distinguishable from its surroundings. As its name suggests, swimming crabs are efficient swimmers and, unlike many other species of crabs, spend their life cycles under water, unless they are accidentally washed ashore or exposed by low tide.

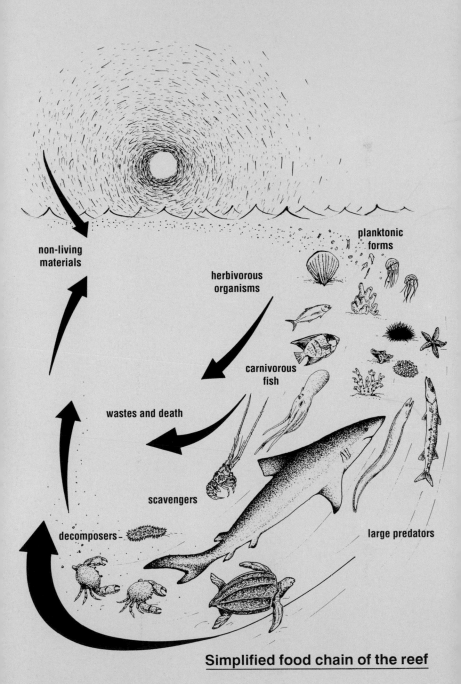

non-living
materials

planktonic
forms

herbivorous
organisms

carnivorous
fish

wastes and death

scavengers

decomposers

large predators

Simplified food chain of the reef

MAJOR GROUPS OF MARINE ANIMALS

PHYLUM	SUB-PHYLUM	CLASS
Porifera (sponges)		Calcarea Demospongiae Sclerospongiae Hexactinellida
Cnidaria	Anthozoa Hydrozoa Scyphozoa	Zoantharia Octocorallia (Stinging Hydroids) (Fire Coral) (Jellyfish)
Platyhelminthes (flatworms)		Turbellaria
Annelida (segmented worms)		Polyohaeta Myzostomaria Oligochaeta
Crustacea		Cephalocarida Branchiopoda Ostracoda Copepoda Branchiura Cirripedia Malacostrace
Mollusca		Monoplacophora Polyplacophora Aplacophora Gastropoda Bivalvia Scaphopoda Cephalopoda
Bryozoa		Phylactolaemata Stenolaemata Gymnolaemata
Echinodermata		Crinoidea Asteroidea Ophiuriodea Echinoidea Holothurioidea
Chordata	Urochordata Cephalochordata Vertebrata	Ascidiacea Thaliacea Larvacea Chondrichthyes (Elasmobranchs) Osteichthyes (Bony fish) Reptilia Mammalia

Not all Phyla are included In this list, only the main groups which divers and snorkellers are likely to see.

Plankton-feeding Fish
Small plankton-eating fish such as these gather in large numbers in areas of the reef which combines a strong current with rich coral growth. The current provides a source of food while the corals provide shelter from predators.

BUILDERS OF THE REEF

Stony corals, soft corals, horny corals, fire corals, precious corals and their near relatives – sea anemones, hydroids and jellyfish – are all members of the Phylum Cnidaria (formerly known as Phylum Coelenterata). Cnidarians are simple, multi-celled organisms. Existing in solitary form or in colonies, Cnidarians have a basic body structure common across species consisting of a radially symmetrical, fleshy sac with a ring of tentacles encircling a single opening located at the sac's apex. Also characteristic of Cnidarians are the stinging cells or nematocysts present on the surface tissue of the tentacles encircling the mouth.

STRUCTURE OF NEMATOCYSTS

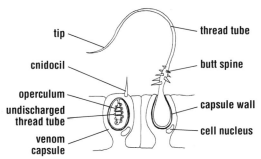

tip

cnidocil

operculum

undischarged
thread tube

venom
capsule

thread tube

butt spine

capsule wall

cell nucleus

Nematocysts are specialised stinging capsules in the outer or surface tissue of the tentacles of Cnidarians. They consist of an inverted barbed thread connected to a venom sac. Often, a small trigger-like structure (cnidocil) acts as the receptor for the physical stimulus that discharges the nematocyst. Once discharged, the venom is delivered along a groove which runs along the thread. The venom is strong enough to kill or paralyse the prey rendering it suitable for ingestion.

The toxins vary greatly from milder forms (such as those of corals) to more dangerous forms, such as that of the deadly Portuguese man-of-war jellyfish. Although nematocyst stings are generally not fatal to human beings, there are exceptions. The venom of the box jellyfish (*Cubomedusae sp.*) and the sea wasp (*Chironex fleckeri*) have caused deaths. Venom from other less lethal species of Cnidarians can cause great discomfort.

HARD CORALS

The stony or hard corals belong to the subphylum Anthozoa and they are the prime builders of massive stony coral reefs. Stony corals are also the most numerous and the most diverse of coral groups. They can be found in a variety of growth forms which, for descriptive purposes, may be described as solitary, massive, encrusting, branching and plate corals.

There are countless genera of hard corals and the majority of them live as colonies containing thousands of small polyps. The coral polyps survive by feeding on the zooplankton present in seawater. As the polyp feeds, the zooplankton is swept into the mouth with the help of the tentacles and, after digestion takes place, the waste products are expelled through the same single opening.

Over the course of their evolution, the stony reef building corals have developed an amazing symbiotic relationship with a group of single-celled algae called zooxanthellae. The algae invade the tissue of the developing coral polyps and immediately begin to reproduce

BASIC STRUCTURE OF CORALS

tentacle

corallite

septa

columella

a)   b)   c)

a) expanded coral polyp   b) withdrawn coral polyp   c) empty coral cup or corallite

to establish their numbers. As they reproduce, the algae are continuously carrying out their food-making activity (photosynthesis).

As tiny plants, algal cells possess structures called chloroplasts which contain complex molecules of a pigment called chlorophyll. In the presence of carbon dioxide and water, chlorophyll traps the sun's energy to manufacture food substances in the form of carbohydrates. Most of the carbohydrate substances manufactured are then passed on to the coral host. This chemical process of photosynthesis and the extra source of food it supplies is instrumental in the impressive reef-building capacity of the stony corals.

STRUCTURE OF A CORAL POLYP

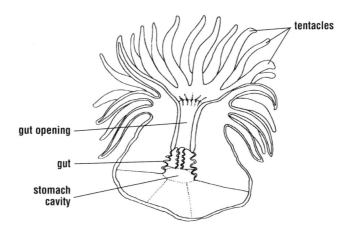

tentacles

gut opening

gut

stomach cavity

Corals may reproduce asexually or sexually. In the asexual method (known as budding), the polyp divides into two. Sexual reproduction occurs when male and female polyps spawn reproductive cells into the water and fertilisation takes place. The planula larvae resulting from the fertilisation continue to develop while drifting in the water. They eventually settle on the reef and establish their own colony.

CORAL GROWTH BY BUDDING

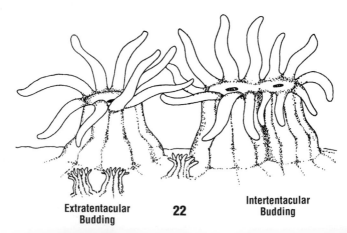

Extratentacular Budding

Intertentacular Budding

Mushroom Coral (*Fungi sp.*)

Mushroom coral is so called because its ribbed surface is similar to the radially arranged gills on the underside of mushrooms. On the reef, species of *Fungia* are often seen scattered between small coral knolls or in an area where coral rubble has collected. Their shape may be discoid or elongate and because some can reach a diameter of 30 cm, they are considered giants among the solitary corals.

There is a large number of species in this genus but they all have similar life cycle and habitats. They start their life as small polyps attached to a stalk, but, as they mature, they break off from the stalk and become free living.

Mushroom corals are very efficient at clearing the sand and sediment that inevitably settle on their upper surfaces. This function enables them to survive as free living organisms in an environment where the constantly shifting rubble or sand might cover and bury them for ever.

Mushroom Coral (*Fungia sp.*)
Fungia reproduce by growing a central stalk which ends in a tiny disc. The disc becomes a 'daughter' polyp that secretes its own skeleton and breaks off to become solitary and free-living.

Close-up of Mushroom Coral (*Fungia sp.*)
The ridges seen here at close range are the corallite septa which have divided repeatedly giving the appearance of the gills on the underside of a mushroom. Numerous tentacles protrude through the ridges when the organism feeds.

Staghorn Coral (*Acropora sp.*)

Staghorn coral is a common hard coral to be found in more sheltered areas of the reef. Because of their distinctive growth pattern, they are also one of the easiest corals to identify.

As its name suggests, staghorn coral grows in a branching formation which resembles stags' horns. They can also be identified by their tubular coral cups or corallites which protrude like pimples about 1-2 mm outwards from the surface of the coral. This feature distinguishes the staghorn coral from other branching corals.

Large areas of staghorn resemble bushy shrub. The protection they afford to other organisms makes them an invaluable part of the reef's ecosystem. Because the tips of staghorn branches are brittle and break off at the slightest touch, staghorns thrive best in reef areas where they will not be lashed by waves.

Staghorn Coral (*Acropora sp.*)
The family Acroporidae consists of many types of coral, some of which form branching bush-like growths commonly called staghorn corals. The numerous spaces between the branches form an excellent hiding place for invertebrates and small fish.

Staghorn Coral in Tiered Growth Form
Table-like staghorn corals are dramatic architects of the reef, exhibiting attractive growth forms resembling multi-storey, shelf-like structures.

Daisy Boulder Coral (*Goniopora sp.*)
This coral colony forms small boulders measuring about 120 cm across. The tubular corallites protrudes from the boulder. When the polyps are feeding the long-stalked polyps emerge from the corallites.

Daisy Boulder Coral (*Goniopora sp.*)

The daisy coral is a favourite of many divers because not only are the polyps expanded by day, but they are so large the general structure of a polyp can be readily detected. The polyps resemble a cluster of sea anemones and each polyp sits in a skeletal cup called a corallite.

Empty corallites are visible in dead parts of the coral reef. Inside each little empty cup calcified plates (called septa) radiate like spokes from an axle. The number and arrangement of these plates is important in precise identification of members of *Goniopora*.

Massive Boulder Bommies (*Porites*)
Some members of the genus *Porites* construct massive towering colonies known as 'bommies'. These structures provide homes for many types of invertebrates, most notably bivalves and annelid tube-worms. The colonies in this picture are estimated to be several hundred years old.

Boulder Coral (*Goniastrea sp.*)
Boulder corals like *Goniastrea*, can be found in large solid boulders or encrusting areas of dead coral.

Plate Coral (*Turbinaria sp.*)
Turbinaria sp. is a type of plate coral which is to be found in deeper waters where light conditions are diminished.

Brain Coral

Colonies of brain coral grow in rounded boulders on the floor of the reef. Labyrinth-like convolutions like those of the human brain cover the exposed surface. Each of the numerous walled compartments in the labyrinth houses a single elongated polyp with many mouths. These massive hermatypic corals are bulwarks of the reef.

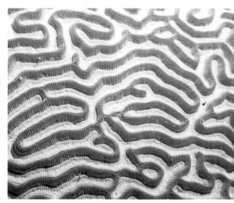

Brain Coral
The colonies of brain corals form by intratentacular budding. The polyps of this particular specimen are withdrawn but the septa are visible.

Bubble Coral (*Plerogyra sp.*)
The polyp of bubble corals expand dramatically during the day, probably for protection and to increase the surface area available for photosynthesis. When the polyps are in this state, they appear more like soft corals than hard corals.

26

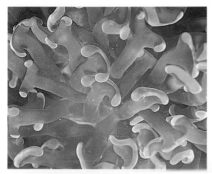

Anchor Coral (*Euphyllia sp.*)
Related to the bubble coral, the tips of the green polyp tentacles of this coral are anchor-shaped in their distended form.

Encrusting Coral
This encrusting coral is composed of three thin sections spreading out in different directions. Encrusting corals are capable of rapidly colonising substantial areas of the reef.

Tree Coral (*Dendrophyllia sp.*)

Dendrophyllia are sometimes called tree corals because of their branching structure. The genus has a large variety of member species, many of which have large conspicuous polyps. In the species shown here, the corallites protrude from the surface of the branches and the polyps are seen in an extended feeding position.

Tree Coral (*Dendrophyllia sp.*)
Dendrophyllia is an attractive, branched coral that bears large polyps at the end of its branches. It grows in deeper waters and can range from dark green to black. It contains no symbiotic algae and is very slow growing.

Cave Coral (*Tubastrea aurea*)

Tubastrea, also known as sun coral, is a fairly common hard coral belonging to the family Dendrophyllidae. They are unusual in their habitat in that they are most commonly found beneath ledges or in locations where they receive little sunlight.

Tubastrea are ahermatypic corals, that is, they do not contain symbiotic algae. Their bright colours are due to the pigment in their tissues. Unlike the hermatypic corals they do not form large colonies or massive skeletons as their only source of nutrition is plankton.

The most common colour of *Tubastrea* is orange, but they can be found in dark green and black as well. Because the individual polyps are so large (reaching up to 1 cm across), they afford an excellent opportunity to closely observe the structure and behaviour of coral polyps.

Cave Coral (*Tubastrea aurea*)
Commonly found in clumps in caves and overhangs, the bright orange *Tubastrea sp.* or cave coral lack the zooxanthellae contained in other corals. They depend on their tentacles to trap and ingest food.

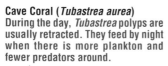

Cave Coral (*Tubastrea aurea*)
During the day, *Tubastrea* polyps are usually retracted. They feed by night when there is more plankton and fewer predators around.

Cave Coral (*Tubastrea aurea*)
Each polyp of *Tubastrea* is about 1 cm in diameter. The central mouth and the surrounding tentacles are clearly visible when the polyps are feeding.

In any ecosystem, hard corals and soft corals, together with many other organisms, exist in profusion competing for available light and space.

OCTOCORALS

Octocorals are a large group of corals which includes **Alcyonarians** (soft corals) and **Gorgonians** (sea fans, sea whips and sea pens). Octocorals distinguish themselves by possessing eight hollow feathery tentacles that surround the mouth of the polyp.

Alcyonarians

Alcyonarians are a group of soft corals belonging to the Order Alcyonacea. Their bodies appear as a fleshy mass which is sometimes branched, but can be lobed. Their bodies lack the stony skeletal structure of the hard corals. Instead, soft corals occur as flabby masses which take on a variety of colours such as dull brown, grey, green, yellow, or violet. Embedded in the fleshy body are polyps which bear eight tentacles.

The soft bodies of these corals are supported by a skeletal structure called spicules. The spicules are embedded in a fleshy gelatinous mass which is covered by a leathery membrane. Deep water alcyonarians are more rigid and contain more spicules. The dense medium of the seawater affords the necessary support to their bodies. When they are removed from the water, their body is so flaccid it will collapse.

Dendronephthya sp.

Dendronephthya are branched and generally white in colour. The colony comes to life and assumes colour when the polyps are extended. The small coralline spicules are denser in appearance than the enclosing body wall and they appear as visible opaque needles embedded in the body mass.

Colonies of this coral may reach a height of over one metre when expanded. The spicules are clearly visible when the colony is contracted. Some species of *Dendronephthya* anchor themselves in sand rather than in the rock. These species have structure that resemble rootlets which help them to maintain a secure hold in the sand.

Dendronephthya sp.
Soft corals like this Dendronephthya specimen appear in a multitude of colours and forms. Despite their flaccid structure, colonies of Dendronephthya can reach more than one metre in height.

Dendronephthya sp.
The detailed structure of Dendronephthya is revealed when part of the colony is observed at close range. The loose distribution of spicules in the branches give them a firm but flexible structure. The polyps are visible when the colony is feeding.

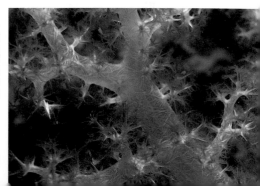

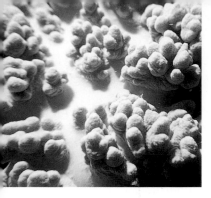

Dead Man's Fingers (*Sinularia sp.*)
Colonies of *Sinularia sp.* often colonise and dominate areas denuded by recent hard coral mortality. They generally grow faster than the hard corals.

Dead Man's Fingers (*Sinularia sp.*)

One of the most frequently occurring soft corals in the Indo-Pacific is the unimpressive greyish-violet lobed mass commonly referred to as 'dead man's fingers'. The surface of *Sinularia* colonies is leathery in texture.

Elephant's Ear Coral (*Sarcophyton sp.*)

Sarcophyton colonies are large, flat, continuous masses. Some can reach up to one metre across. Their convoluted formations give them the appearance of ruffles on a dancer's skirt. The surface of the fleshly colony becomes smooth when the coral polyps are withdrawn.

Elephant's Ear Coral (*Sarcophyton sp.*)
Species of the soft coral sarcophyton grow abundantly in tropical waters. The polyps scattered over the rubbery surface often feed during the day.

Pumping Coral (*Xenia sp.*)
Xenia is an octocoral. It is commonly called pumping coral due to the pulsating action of its polyps.

Octocoral
The eight delicate tentacles of this colonial octocoral have hollow interiors connected with the stomach cavity. The branches are supported by an internal skeleton.

Octocoral
Octocorals are bottom dwellers and some are so delicate that they often go unnoticed. The polyps are fragile and will break off if handled.

Gorgonians

The horny corals or gorgonians are colonies of polyps related to corals. They include familiar species such as sea fans and sea whips. Gorgonians may have an axial skeleton made of calcareous spicules, or a horny skeleton made of gorgonin, or both. Gorgonians grow in abundance in tropical waters and they are found in a wide range of beautiful colours. Their resemblance to plants has led to groups of them being referred to as underwater gardens.

Sea Fan (*Melithaea sp.*)

Sea fan polyps are borne aloft in the current on the flexible branches of the sea fan. The fan usually grows across the prevailing current, so well-developed fans are useful indicators of the strength and direction of water flow. Sea fan polyps are small and are best seen at night, or when the current is strong. When they are fully extended, the tiny polyps bearing eight tentacles are clearly visible.

Other invertebrates may be seen perched on the branches of the sea fan as they seek food carried by the current. Small spider crabs, brittle-stars and certain species of comb jellyfish

Sea Fan (*Melithaea sp.*)
Gorgonians are slow-growing. Mature colonies such as these take many decades to grow.

Sea Fan (*Melithaea sp.*)
Gorgonians are interesting to observe at night when plankton is more abundant and the polyps are feeding.

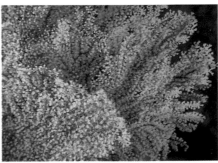

Sea Fan (*Melithaea sp.*)
Sea fans feed on plankton. They flourish in exposed locations such as the edge of the reef where they will grow at any angle to take advantage of the abundant food supply furnished by the currents.

commonly behave in this way. The sea fan is supported by a nodular skeleton. Sea fans are slow growing, but they are an important part of the reef environment. If you bring them to the surface they lose colour, smell terrible, and slowly disintegrate. They are much more beautiful left where they are.

Sea Whip

Sea whips are long, smooth, strand-like colonies of polyps which are less spectacular both in shape and colour than sea fans. They are diverse in form and their body structure is much more flexible than sea fans. Tiny polyps are embedded in the sea whip's body wall but they are only visible when they are feeding. Sea whips may grow in single strands (such as in the genus *Juncella*) or they may take on a branched, candelabra form (as in the genus *Ctenocella*).

Sea Whips
Sea whips are found in poor light conditions in deeper areas of the reef where they often dominate the sea-scape.

Sea Whip
At night, the smooth, stringy surface of sea whips comes alive with polyps. The polyps of sea whips have eight tentacles.

Sea Pen
Resembling a robust feather, sea pens consist of a modified, fleshy central polyp with smaller polyps branching to the side. Some species are quite large, reaching up to one metre in height. The most spectacular species are luminescent. Sea pens grow in shallow, muddy locations and they retract into the mud when disturbed.

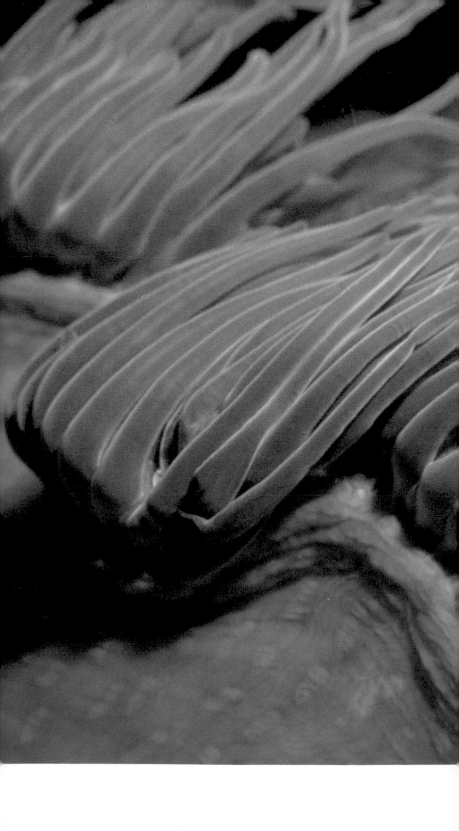

Sea Anemone
The colourful base of the anemone is often obscured by its spreading tentacles.
Here, the tentacles are swept aside by the current. The tentacles of anemone
not only provide a habitat for the familiar anemonefish, but small crabs and
other crustacea are also associated with the sea anemone.

SEA ANEMONES

These solitary, free living, flower-like Cnidarians are grouped with corals because of their many structural similarities. They are closely related to hard, reef-building corals except that they do not secrete calcarious skeletons. Although they remain attached to their substrate most of the time, anemones are capable of moving from place to place by sliding slowly on their base or pedal disc.

The sac-like body of anemones is surprisingly muscular and can contort itself to a variety of shapes. Like their relatives the tiny coral polyps, the single opening or mouth of anemones is situated at the free, upper end of the sac. Encircling the mouth are rings of hollow tentacles which bear thousands of nematocysts. The nematocysts of anemones function in much the same way as those of their relatives by stinging their prey. When threatened, some anemones can withdraw their tentacles completely.

Sea anemones are carnivorous and feed in a similar fashion to the coral polyps, except that they make more deliberate use of their tentacles and capture much larger prey such as fish. As soon as one tentacle detects or comes into contact with a source of food, the signal goes to the other tentacles to follow suit. The tentacles then fasten onto the prey and convey it to the central mouth. After digestion takes place in the gut, the indigestible parts of the food are ejected via the mouth. Sea anemones have surprising longevity. Some species kept in aquaria are reported to have lived for 50-70 years.

Giant Sea Anemone (*Stoichactis sp.*)

The giant sea anemone is the largest of the anemones found along the reef edge. Its enormous disc is an unspectacular shade of brown tinged with green. It can, however, grow to impressive proportions reaching more than one metre in diameter. The expanded disc adheres to the rock by means of adhesive patches in much the same way tacks keep a carpet in place.

Relatives

Giant Sea Anemone (*Stoichactis sp.*)
Giant sea anemones such as *Stoichactis sp.* can grow to an impressive size of more than one metre in diameter.

Common Sea Anemone (*Radianthus sp.*)

Several rings of medium to short tentacles encircle the wavy edge of the disc of *Radianthus*. With its numerous folds, *Radianthus* is a favourite haunt of anemonefish. Anemonefish are able to sustain a commensal relationship with their anemone host over a long period of time. This is possible because of the anemonefish's immunity to the stings of the anemone's nematocysts. This relationship is described in more detail in the 'Special Relationships' section of this guide.

Common Sea Anemone (*Radianthus sp.*)
Like other sea anemones, *Radianthus* or the common sea anemone will close up if threatened by predators or if water conditions are adverse. Anemones are often called flowers of the sea because they brighten up the reef. The group name, *Anthozoa*, means 'flower (*antas*) animal (*zoa*)'.

39

Blobbed Anemone (*Gyrostoma sp.*)
Gyrostoma sp. has unique-shaped tentacles with swollen, bubble-like tips.

Blobbed Sea Anemone (*Gyrostoma sp.*)

Gyrostoma is a smaller species of sea anemone than Radianthus. *Gyrostoma* lives mostly in groups or colonies below tide level, securing itself in rock or coral crevices to which it retreats when threatened.

The most striking characteristic of the genus *Gyrostoma* is the swollen tips at the end of each tentacle. These blobs are circled in white and may diminish or change in size and shape at times. *Gyrostoma* is a popular haunt of anemonefish.

Pimply Sea Anemone (*Actinodiscus sp.*)

Found in deeper waters, this curiously formed anemone lacks the obvious tentacles usually associated with anemones, but its central mouth is easily distinguished. *Actinodiscus* will withdraw its expansive peripheral edges when touched. It then takes on a shape that looks somewhat like an inverted balloon.

Pimply Sea Anemone (*Actinodiscus sp.*)
Actinodiscus has an unusual form for a sea anemone. Its tentacles are fused to form a continuous disc which surrounds the prominent central mouth. The organism often reaches 70cm in diameter.

Pimply Sea Anemone (*Actinodiscus sp.*)
When they withdraw into a defensive position, each retracted pimply sea anemone resembles an inverted balloon.

Banded Tube Anemone (*Pachycerianthus maua*)
Pachycerianthus maua is one of many species of tube
anemones found in tropical waters. Its fine tentacles
are marked with delicate brown bands.

Banded Tube Anemone (*Pachycerianthus maua*)

Most tube anemones can be found buried in the sand or between
rocks. Tube anemones form a mucous tube in which they live. Because
their tubes resemble those of many annelids, they are often confused
with tubeworms. Like tubeworms, they will rapidly withdraw their
tentacles if they are disturbed. *Pachycerianthus maua* is one of the
many tube anemones common to the region and it can be identified
by the outer ring of long, delicately banded tentacles and an inner
ring of shorter, thicker ones.

**Tube Anemone
(*Pachycerianthus sp.*)**
This unidentified tube anemone has
numerous white tentacles which
have a powerful sting.

41

ZOANTHIDEA

These unusual organisms are colonial in form and they typically colonise areas of the reef flat. Their large polyps are sac-like and they arise from a common leathery tissue mass which spreads over the substrate on which the colony is growing. *Zoanthids* can be found encrusting rocks, but they also attach themselves to other organisms such as sponges, dead corals and gorgonians. In common with their relatives the soft corals, their skeleton consists of isolated calcareous spicules.

Zoanthidea
These unusual colonial animals typically colonise areas of the reef flat. Their large polyps are sac-like and they arise from a common leathery tissue mass which spreads over the substrate on which the colony is growing. Zoanthids encrust rocks or attach themselves to other organisms such as sponges, dead corals and gorgonians.

HYDROZOA

The class Hydrozoa consists of approximately 3,000 species, the majority of which are marine. Two groups commonly seen on the reef and described here are the fire corals and the stinging hydroids.

Fire Corals

One group of Cnidaria often confused with true corals are members of the Milleporina, better known as fire corals. Millepores bear a superficial resemblance to true corals in that they exist in a variety of formations such as: a) massive calcareous plates, b) leaf-like or branching structures, or c) encrusting formations covering the surface of rocks and coral heads. The colonies have a dull yellow to brown appearance and the growth regions of the colony are whitish in colour.

Fire corals can be distinguished from true corals by their absence of corallite cups. A close inspection of Millepores will reveal that the surface is relatively smooth with a scattering of millions of minute pores – hence the name 'millepores'. On occasions, the surface appears to be covered by a fuzz of white hair which are actually the tentacles of minute polyps.

Fire Corals
Millepores are stony colonial hydroids that superficially resemble corals (hence their common name) but structurally they are very different. The colonies are invariably a yellow-brown colour and have a smooth surface. The growth regions are a whitish colour.

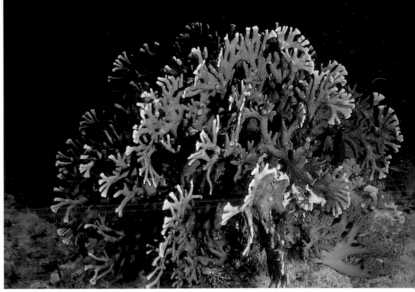

Fire Corals
Millepores are also found in leafy plate-like formations
and are a favourite habitat of clams and tube worms.

The specialised stinging cells of fire coral are much more powerful than those of other types of corals. They are likely, on contact, to cause an uncomfortable burn on the skin.

Fire coral usually grows in exposed areas of the reef where there is considerable water movement. They are often found in shallow water around reef edges. These are precisely the most likely conditions for accidental contact by swimmers or divers.

Branched Fire Coral
A close inspection of the smooth surface of Millepores will reveal that the colony is the stronghold of millions of tiny polyps which, when they protrude their tentacles, give a fuzzy appearance to the colony. Though tiny, the tentacles of these polyps have nematocysts that can render a powerful sting.

Stinging Hydroids

Aglaophenia is a brownish-pink, colonial hydroid common to the Indo-Pacific region. It is found on the reef slope attached to the rocks and corals. Its growth form resembles ferns with branches reaching to up 20 cm in height.

Aglaophenia's common name 'sea nettle' refers to the fact that it can inflict the same degree of discomfort as its namesake on land. If it accidently contacts the skin, welts appear immediately and severe

itching results. These welts may develop into blisters and take a few weeks to subside.

Aglaophenia is closely related to *Lytocarpus*, another stinging nettle which is described in the 'Marine Animals to Avoid' section of this guide.

Stinging Hydroid (*Aglaophenia sp.*)
Species of *Aglaophenia* grow in fern-like formations reaching up to 20 cm in length. If touched, it causes a painful, burning sting resulting in an itchy rash and weals which last a week or two.

Sea Nettle (*Lytocarpus sp.*)
Lytocarpus is a smaller branching stinging hydroid but its sting is equally painful. Its fine structure makes it difficult to see, especially at the mouths of caves or in crevices where it is often found.

Sea Nettles
Sea nettles are delicate and sometimes difficult to see in poor light conditions such as in caves. Contact with sea nettle branches can cause an unpleasant sting for the unwary.

JELLYFISH

Jellyfish are coral relatives which are free-living medusoid forms of the Subphylum Medusozoa. Along with other Cnidarians, jellyfish are known for their stinging cells which are located primarily on their tentacles. Jellyfish range from microscopic in size to enormous dimensions.

Jellyfish have two main parts to their body: the umbrella-shaped body or bell and the tentacles. The bell of jellyfish is a gelatinous mass which is most often translucent but can be tinted with purple, green or brown. Jellyfish propel themselves by rhythmic pulsations of the bell. Movement is created as water is pushed out of the concave space under the bell. Although they can float to the surface or move horizontally, jellyfish are unable to overcome tides or currents which often deposit them on shore. Thus, jellyfish can also be considered plankton since they are technically 'drifting' organisms.

The mouth of the jellyfish is centrally located at the end of a projection (the manubrium) which hangs down from the centre of the underside of the bell. Near the margin of the bell and sometimes forming a fringe arising from the manubrium are tentacles armed with the microscopic stinging nematocysts. When a small animal

Jellyfish
The tentacles of a jellyfish originate from the underside of the bell. The manubrium also protrudes from the underside of the bell rather like the handle of an umbrella. Often, the most conspicuous features are the reproductive and digestive organs which can be observed through the transparent bell.

Lion's mane Jellyfish
The bowl-shaped bell of the lion's mane jellyfish has scalloped margins and it is seen here from the top in its extended position. Reaching up to one metre in diameter, it is large and bulky when compared to the bell of other jellyfish. The lion's mane jellyfish is often found in coastal areas. It should be observed at a distance, however, as it has a powerful sting.

brushes against them, the nematocysts eject fine hollow threads that pierce the animal's skin. Venomous substances then flow down a canal located in the core of each thread to paralyse the victim on contact.

Jellyfish feed on small fish and shrimps which swim near the surface. The released nematocyst threads not only paralyse the prey but hold it firmly in place. The more the prey struggles, the more securely it becomes trapped as it comes into contact with still more nematocysts, which, in turn, shoot out their venomous threads.

Digestion takes place in the gut cavity inside the bell. Digestive juices flow into the gut and reduce the prey to a soupy substance, causing the bell to turn opaque.

Lion's Mane Jellyfish
The tentacles of the lion's mane jellyfish are as spectacular as its bell. In mature specimens, the finer tentacles reach a length of 10 metres. The centrally located mouth on the underside of the bell is drawn out into four long, frilled lobes resembling a lion's mane — hence its common name.

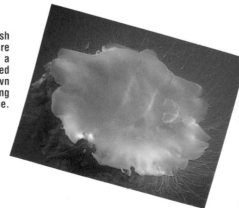

Pink Coralline Algae
Effective as reef builders, encrusting pink coralline algae help to stabilise loose rocks and rubble on the reef.

ALGAE

Forming an important part of life on the reef are numerous species of marine algae. Apart from the microscopic, one-celled algae that inhabit the cells of other organisms or make up a major proportion of plankton life, more conspicuous forms such as species of green and brown algae commonly recognised as seaweeds can be found colonising rocks, particularly in the intertidal zone. Adaptive features such as their anchor or holdfast and their tough, leathery outer surface ensure their survival in this unstable region. The luxuriant growth forms of most of these seaweeds provide a valuable source of food and a protective hiding place for small invertebrate organisms. Also present on the reef are encrusting colonies of coralline algae.

Coralline algae incorporate calcium carbonate into their cell walls as they grow over the surface of rocks and dead coral. Thus they bind together loose rocks and rubble helping to stabilise areas of the reef. Common among the coralline algae are the pink or red types which, because of their attractive colour and variety of growth forms, are often mistaken for coral.

Halimeda sp.
Halimeda is a calcified green algae which appears in clumps clinging to rocks on the reef flat. Each clump is composed of strings of flattened, fan-shaped segments which are hardy enough to survive intermittent exposure to sunlight as well as the rough action of waves.

Brown Algae
Brown algae often grow in masses of long, leathery strap-shaped structures called fronds. Algae colonies provide a haven for small invertebrates such as crustaceans and molluscs.

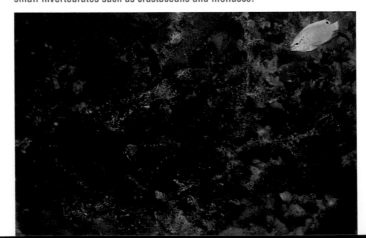

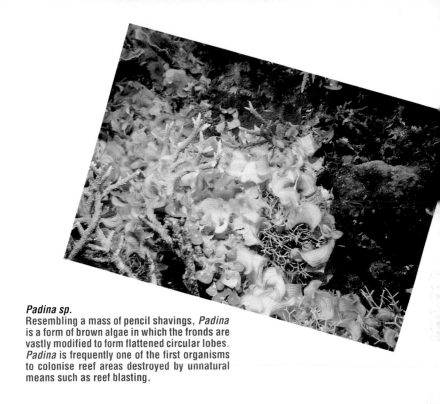

Padina sp.
Resembling a mass of pencil shavings, *Padina*
is a form of brown algae in which the fronds are
vastly modified to form flattened circular lobes.
Padina is frequently one of the first organisms
to colonise reef areas destroyed by unnatural
means such as reef blasting.

Padina sp.
In some species of *Padina*, concentric growth
lines are clearly visible in the semicircular or
circular lobes.

Painted Sweetlips (*Plectorhycus pictus*)
Territorial in nature, the painted sweetlips is often found esconced in a coral crevice close to shallow areas with sandy or muddy substrates. In such a location, it lies in wait for unsuspecting prey which can be efficiently disposed of in the fish's powerful jaws. The adult painted sweetlips grows to a length of about 90 cms.

Fish are the coral reef's most highly-developed and most dominant form of life. Fish that inhabit coral reefs exist in virtually every conceivable colour, shape and form. Reef fish also exhibit almost every type of adaptation for movement, feeding, defence and reproduction.

Generally speaking, reef fishes are smaller, more compact, and have broader tails and stubbier fins than their open water relatives. Thus they are able to make abrupt turns and rapid starts and stops in and out of the many nooks and crannies of the reef. Because of the large numbers of fish living together on the reef (many of which prey on their neighbours), responsiveness and mobility are a key to survival.

But regardless of their size and form, almost all species of reef fish display colours and patterns of boldness and brilliance that are stunning. Colouration plays a number of roles in the survival of individual fish. Initially, colouration provides camouflage against the background of corals by concealing the fish and confusing predators. Colouration together with markings also aid in mutual recognition of like-species prior to courtship. This may be one explanation of why juvenile forms of many species are much less colourful than their adult forms. Juveniles do not need to be recognised by a potential mate and, at the same time, subtle colouration provides them with camouflage when they need it most.

There is also great diversity in defence mechanisms among reef fish. Some fish are well-camouflaged by their colour, while others rely on immobility for protection. Yet others have an arsenal of injurious or venomous spines.

Reproductive patterns of fish take on a wide range of forms. In the majority of species of reef fish, fertilisation takes place externally, eggs are laid seasonally, and eggs and offspring are usually not nurtured by the female.

Larger fish are less dependent on the reef for shelter and protection but depend on the reef as a source of food. These larger fish include sharks, rays and barracuda, which are seen more often in open waters at the fringe of the reef, even by day.

Large predatory fish might be called masters of the reef in that they are at the apex of the food pyramid. Formidable predators such as sharks and barracuda kill only what they need to eat so there is neither waste nor deliberate cruelty in their killing.

Fish are aquatic cold-blooded vertebrates. Their diversity and success in aquatic environments is due, in part, to their efficient, specialised breathing mechanism. Breathing takes place as water is taken in through the mouth, passed over the filamentous gills, and discharged through openings which lie behind the eye. An exchange of oxygen and carbon dioxide occurs through the thin capillary walls of the gill filaments. In most fish, the gills are covered by a large conspicuous flap called an operculum.

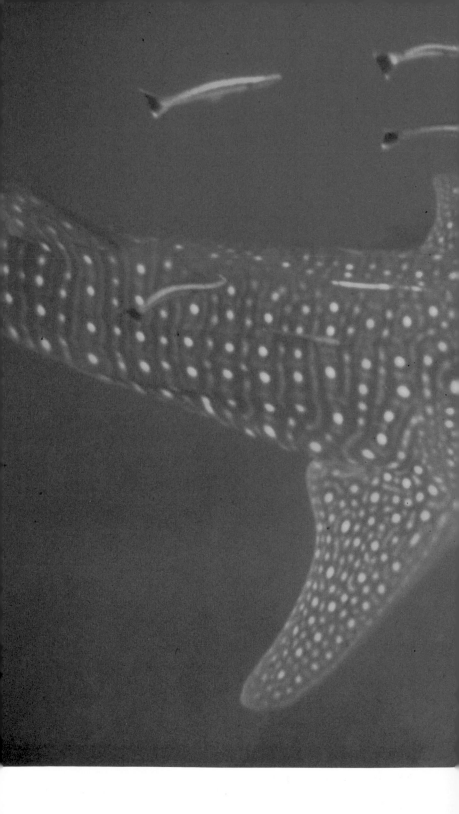

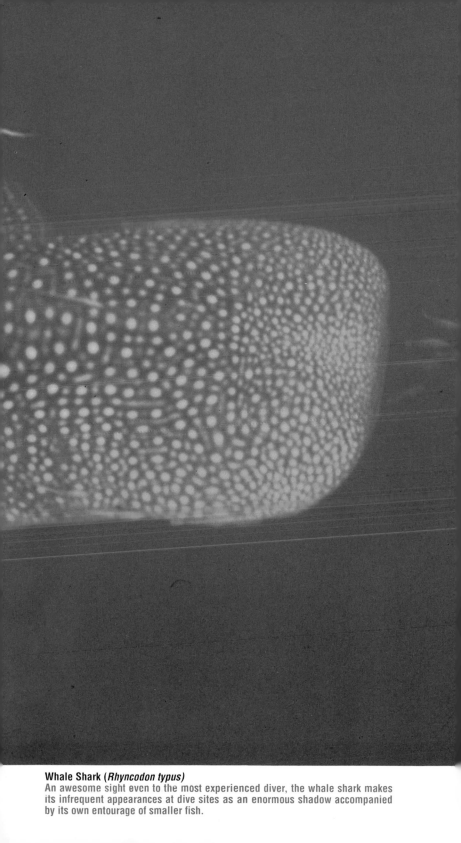

Whale Shark (*Rhyncodon typus*)
An awesome sight even to the most experienced diver, the whale shark makes its infrequent appearances at dive sites as an enormous shadow accompanied by its own entourage of smaller fish.

As a rule, the head and body of the fish are not distinctly separated. The body shape varies according to the habitat and way of life of the fish. Generally, fish fit into four basic categories as far as body shape is concerned: a) compressed from side to side as in most reef species (such as angelfish and butterflyfish); b) flattened from top to bottom (as in the rays); c) spindle shaped to facilitate rapid movement in open water (viz. barracuda and tuna); d) long, slender and snake-like to fit into crevices (such as the eels).

The majority of fish are equipped with a scaly skin, a mucous coating and at least one type of fin. The scales are of various forms and sizes but they are arranged so that they overlap to form a firm, protective cover. The slippery mucous coating which envelops the fish serves several purposes. The mucous substance prevents or minimizes infestation by parasites and it seals the fish's body fluids ensuring that they are not diluted by their watery surroundings. The mucous covering also reduces friction so that the fish is able to move through water with ease.

Most fish possess fins on various parts of their body. Fins are required for locomotion, balance, stabilisation and directional change. Fins can take on a variety of sizes and shapes according to the function they perform. Fins can be hard-rayed and spiny or they can be soft-rayed. The number and form of rays in the fins (particularly in the dorsal fin) is a feature that distinguishes one species of fish from another.

The external features of fish are closely linked with the type of skeletal structure they possess. In this respect, fish fall into two major categories. The skeleton may be cartilaginous as in the sharks and rays, or it may be bony, as in the case of about 95 per cent of fish species found on the reef. Bony fish range in size from large fish such as barracuda and jackfish to tiny fish such as damsels.

Kingfish (*Rachycentron sp.*)
The kingfish or cobia is built for life in the open sea. Its streamlined body can reach two metres in length and weigh up to 50 kg (which was the 'modest' estimate of the photographer who submitted this picture!).

SHARKS AND RAYS

Sharks and rays are cartilaginous fish that belong to an ancient group of fish known as elasmobranchs. The basic physiology of elasmobranchs has changed very little over the past 200 million years since they appeared on the evolutionary scale. Like all other fish, elasmobranchs breathe through gills which are associated with external openings called gill slits. Depending on the species, five to seven pairs of gill slits are visible behind the eye. Unlike bony fish, however, the gill slits of elasmobranchs are not covered by a gill flap or operculum.

Grey Reef Shark (*Carcharhinus sp.*)
The grey reef shark frequents open water but occasionally visits the reef. It is seen here in open water swallowing a piece of fish that was fed to it by a diver. This species has been implicated in a number of shark attacks.

Manta Ray (*Manta sp.*)
Mantas are the giants of all rays. The Pacific manta can reach a body span of 6 metres and weight of 1,600 kg. Mantas are true inhabitants of the open sea and can travel at great speed. They visit the reef occasionally where they can sometimes be seen cruising around or floating motionless while they are being denuded of parasites by attentive cleanerfish.

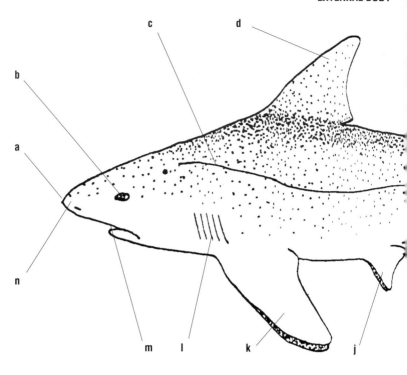

Apart from having a skeleton composed of cartilage rather than bone, elasmobranchs differ from the majority of fish species in that, instead of having scales, their skin is protected by primitive placoid structures called denticles. The serrated, free edges of the denticles give shark skin its abrasive texture. Denticles are enlarged and modified in the mouth region. In many species of sharks they form rows of formidable slanting teeth. Shark skin is sometimes used commercially in making shoes and, because of its rough texture, it has been used for generations as a natural abrasive.

There are over 200 species of sharks. They range in size from a tiny 60 cm dogfish to the largest of all fish: the whale shark. These enormous plankton feeders can reach a length of 20 metres. Despite their enormous size, however, whale sharks are relatively harmless.

Sharks are a successful group because their acute predatory senses make them effective hunters. With the exception of the whale sharks and basking sharks, some large species are regarded as dangerous to humans and consequently they are subjects of suspicion and fear worldwide.

Black-tip Reef Shark (*Carcharhinus melanopterus*)

One of the most graceful and well-proportioned of all sharks, the black-tip reef shark's body colouration is beige or greyish with a lighter lateral streak originating from the anal fin. It can be identified immediately by the prominent black tips on all fins. The most

FEATURES OF A SHARK

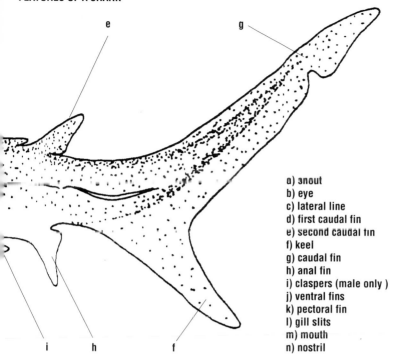

a) snout
b) eye
c) lateral line
d) first caudal fin
e) second caudal fin
f) keel
g) caudal fin
h) anal fin
i) claspers (male only)
j) ventral fins
k) pectoral fin
l) gill slits
m) mouth
n) nostril

prominent marking is on the first dorsal fin. The trailing edge of the tail fin is also fringed with black, as is its lower lobe. A shallow water predator, the black-tip can be seen at the edge of the reef where it feeds mostly on bony fish. It is generally considered a scavenger but, when attacking prey, it is fast and aggressive.

Many species of sharks that feed at night have well-developed eyes that enable them to see even in dim light. Behind the retina of the eye are specialised cells that act like mirrors. Light striking these cells is immediately reflected to other cells, thus multiplying the visual effect. Under normal conditions, the black-tip is easily frightened and stays well clear of divers. Occasionally, however, there are reports of discrepant behaviour among black-tips which have been seen to pester divers in mid-water or at the surface.

Black-tip Reef Shark
(*Carcharhinus melanopterus*)
Occasional visitors to offshore reefs, the graceful black-tip reef shark is a retiring species. This fairly young captive specimen was photographed in a lagoon.

63

White-tip Reef Shark
(*Triaenodon obesus*)
The slender bodied white-tip usually keeps its distance from divers but can be pugnacious when feeding. The white-tip is one of the few sharks that does not need to swim in order to pump water through its gills. It is occasionally seen motionless in sheltered sandy areas close to the reef edge.

White-tip Reef Shark (*Triaenodon obesus*)

As its name suggests, the white-tip reef shark can be identified by conspicuous white tips on the dorsal fin and on the upper lobe of the tail fin. The head of the white-tip is flattened and its snout blunted. Also conspicuous are ridges above the eyes and the prominent nasal flaps. The length of the white-tip rarely exceeds 1.5 metres and juveniles of around one metre are common on reefs in the South China Sea.

The white-tip reef shark feeds at night in shallow waters, especially if there is a slack tide. They are bottom feeders exploring cracks and crevices where they can corner small fish or octopus. White-tips appear to have poor eyesight and they hunt mainly by smell.

White-tips are capable of respiring as they lie passively at rest in caves or on the sandy bottom of shallow, sheltered areas. They sometimes take residence in a particular cave and may frequent the same cave for months or, in some cases, years.

Indo-Pacific Nurse Shark (*Nebrius concolor*)

The greyish or beige-coloured Indo-Pacific nurse shark is easily identified by a sail-shaped dorsal fin set unusually far back above the pelvic region. Its tail fin has a much-reduced lower lobe and flanking its mouth are fleshy barbels which protrude downwards in front of each nostril. Like most other species of sharks, nurse sharks are a lighter colour on their ventral surface.

The Indo-Pacific nurse shark is nocturnal and can be seen at night slowly and deliberately foraging for food on the reef. Although they have powerful jaws, the diet of nurse sharks consists mainly of small reef invertebrates such as sea urchins, crabs and octopus. Nurse sharks are also noted for their peculiar form of suction feeding. They place their mouths close to their prey and create a vacuum sufficient to suck the victim into their mouth.

The Indo-Pacific nurse shark is not considered aggressive, but they are actively defensive. As is true for all sharks, nurse sharks are reluctant to let go once they have bitten. So, even though nurse sharks look passive enough as they 'dream' away the day, it is wise not to disturb their slumber!

Indo-Pacific Nurse Shark
(*Nebrius concolor*)
Like the white-tip, the nurse shark is able to keep water flowing through its gills while it is stationary. During the day nurse sharks remain in a lethargic state in shallow caves or under rock ledges.

Indo-Pacific Nurse Shark
(*Nebrius concolor*)
It is wise not to disturb resting nurse sharks — even when they appear to be in deep slumber — they are reluctant to let go once they have bitten.

Juvenile Nurse Shark
(*Nebrius concolor*)
The prominent nasal flaps and barbels of this juvenile nurse shark are clearly visible in this photograph. Juveniles have pointed snouts and proportionately longer barbels than adults.

Leopard Shark (*Stegostoma fasciatum*)

The leopard shark can sometimes be seen in shallow waters in the South China Sea. Recognizable by their spots and their blunt nose, leopard sharks are relatively shy. They can be seen most often at dusk searching the sea bed for molluscs and crustaceans.

Young leopard sharks have quite a different colouration from adults. They are sometimes mistakenly referred to as zebra sharks because their black or dark purple body has lighter stripes. Leopard sharks appear to be rather docile. If observed from a distance, they are usually not aggressive towards divers.

Leopard Shark (*Stegostoma fasciatum*)
Recognisable by their spots and their blunt nose, leopard sharks are relatively shy. During the early evening they search the sea bed for molluscs and crustaceans.

Whale Shark (*Rhincodon typus*)

Reaching a maximum of 18 metres in length and 41,000 kilograms in weight, the whale shark is reported to be the world's largest living species of fish. Despite its formidable appearance, whale sharks are plankton feeders and therefore pose only a negligible threat to divers. In fact, some researchers even report that whale sharks playfully welcome the close attention of divers.

Whale Shark (*Rhincodon typus*)

The whale shark feeds by swimming at its normal pace with its mouth wide open. Water thus swept into the mouth is strained through the spongy gill tissues and anything too large to pass through is consumed. Apart from the usual planktonic forms present in the water, small fish and pelagic invertebrates such as squid comprise the whale shark's diet.

Whale Shark (*Rhincodon typus*)

In this dorsal view, the pattern of dorsal markings and the broad anterior snout are clearly visible.

Manta Ray (*Manta sp.*)

Also known as 'devil rays', mantas are relatives of sharks. The body structure and colouration of mantas (a dorso-ventrally flattened body which is dark on top and light underneath) suggests that they have evolved from being bottom feeders to feeding in mid-water.

Apart from their enormous size, the most striking feature of the manta is the palps which are located on both sides of the mouth. These lobe-like structures direct the current inwards, sweeping sea water containing small fish and plankton into the ventral mouth. Thereafter, the abundantly supplied water flows through strainers located adjacent to the gills.

Not much is known about the reproductive habits of mantas except that fertilisation is internal. Female mantas retain the fertilised eggs inside their bodies and the young are born at a fairly advanced stage of development.

Mantas are frequently accompanied by an entourage of fish including remoras which attach themselves to the manta's body for a 'free ride'. Mantas are not aggressive but, due to their enormous size, divers are advised to avoid getting in their way!

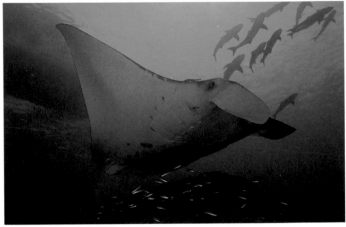

Manta Ray (*Manta sp.*)
In this photograph the structure of the manta's palps is clearly visible. Mantas typically travel with an entourage of smaller fish. The fish seen here are taking advantage of the water currents around the mouth of the manta.

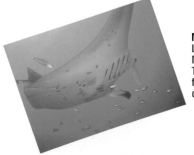

Manta Ray (*Manta sp.*)
Large female mantas can often be seen in Malaysian waters at Magiciennes Rock or around Tekong Bahara. Males are distinguishable from females by their modified anal fins which form cylindrical copulatory organs called claspers.

Spotted Eagle Ray (*Aetobatus narinari*)
Although pelagic in nature, eagle rays are bottom feeders. They probe in the sand for molluscs and crustaceans which they are able to crush effectively with their powerful teeth.

Spotted Eagle Ray (*Aetobatus narinari*)

Like the bird after which they are named, the movements of eagle rays are a picture of swiftness and grace. They are notorious jumpers and, for reasons that are not clearly understood, will sometimes burst forth from the surface of the water in a giant leap. Including the long slender tail, the total body length of an adult spotted eagle ray can reach more than two metres.

Although they are pelagic in nature, eagle rays are bottom feeders, probing in the sand for molluscs and crustaceans which they are able to crush effectively with their powerful jaws. They often travel in groups of four or five. Because of their voracious appetite, they can be extremely destructive to commercial oyster and clam beds.

Blue-spotted Lagoon Ray (Taeniura Iymma)

This attractive ray, notable for its exquisite bright blue markings on a dull green body, is the most common stingray found on reefs in the South China Sea. In fact, when you see a cloud of silt in the water, it could well be the sign of a blue-spotted lagoon ray searching for its prey.

Blue-spotted Lagoon Ray
(*Taeniura Iymma*)
In a characteristic pose, this blue-spotted lagoon ray has retreated under a ledge. Note that the eyes are located on bumps on the dorsal surface of the body. This allows the eyes of a buried lagoon ray to protrude sufficiently to keep track of what goes on around it.

The gills of all rays are located on the underside of the body. Gills are used to good effect when rays search for their prey. A stream of water spurts from the gills while at the same time, rays flap their pectoral fins close to the surface of the sea bed. Thus they are able to uncover food sources such as clams and sea urchins that might be hiding in the debris on the sea bed. Like other stingrays, blue-spotted lagoon rays have powerful grinding teeth which allow them to break up shells and other protective coverings of their prey.

Because the lagoon ray is very shy and usually remains hidden under ledges when divers are around, there is little chance of stepping on one by accident. Nevertheless, divers and snorkellers should keep in mind that extremely potent venom is stored in paired grooves running the length of two poison spines located part way along the tail.

Blue-spotted Lagoon Ray (*Taeniura lymma*)
With its posterior end facing the camera, the dimensions of the tail of the blue-spotted lagoon ray become apparent. The length of the tail exceeds the diameter of the disc making the total length of an adult ray up to two metres in length.

Electric Ray (*Hypnos sp.*)
The dorso-ventrally flattened body of the electric ray is evidence that
it is a bottom feeder. However, their small jaws would be ineffective
in catching large prey and this is where the ability of the electric ray
to emit an electrical discharge comes in useful. The electric shock
stuns larger prey making them an easy kill.

Electric Ray (*Hypnos sp.*)

Electric rays can be found in tropical, subtropical, as well as temperate seas. Several Indo-Pacific species frequent the shallow waters
of fringing coral reefs. Electric rays are, however, sighted only infrequently due to their highly effective camouflage and their habit of
remaining partially buried in the sand.

The electric ray uses its capacity to emit electrical discharges to
good effect when hunting for food. The prey is first forced downwards in the direction of the sea bed and is promptly enveloped
within the ray's wide, ovate pectoral fins. The ray then emits an
electrical discharge which either kills or stuns the prey, rendering
it suitable for eating. Without this facility, electric rays, which possess small jaws, would not be able to catch substantially-sized prey.

The electric discharge given off by the electric rays was well-known
by the Greeks who used electric ray shock treatment as a cure for
a range of ailments such as headache, mental illness and gout.

Giant Stingray (*Dasyatis brevicaudata*)
This large species of stingray has a circular disc
which is black on the dorsal surface and white
underneath. Note the elevated eyes on the dorsal
surface, the cusp-shaped mouth and paired gill
slits which are located on the ventral surface.

LARGE BONY REEF FISH

As their name suggests, bony fish have a skeleton made of bone. Their skeleton consists of a backbone or spinal column to which the locomotory organs or fins are attached. The number, position, size and shape of the fins vary greatly from one fish to another. Generally speaking, the more closely related the species, the more similar the fin structure is likely to be. Many bony fish have well-developed, specialised fins which make them excellent swimmers. Large pelagic fish such as tuna swim at impressive speeds over long distances.

The skin of most bony fish is a thick dermal layer embedded with flat overlapping scales which are arranged rather like tiles on a roof. These scales grow larger as the fish matures and in temperate species seasonal rings on the scales will reveal the age of the fish.

Most bony fish reproduce by external fertilisation. Eggs are released from the ovary and expelled as millions of jelly-coated spheres. Similarly, the male sperm are also discharged in their millions. Not all the eggs are fertilized, but even those that are have high prospects of falling prey to other organisms before they hatch.

A unique internal feature of most bony fish is the swim bladder. Although the precise mechanism of the swim bladder is not fully understood, it is believed to have an auditory as well as a buoyancy control function.

Jack (*Caranx sp.*)
Jacks are more often found in open water but are occasional visitors to the reef since they follow the current as they feed. Their body is compressed and a bright silvery colour.

EXTERNAL BODY FEATURES OF A BONY FISH

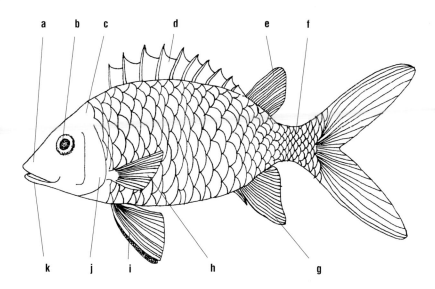

a) nostril   b) eye   c) nape   d) first dorsal fin
e) second dorsal fin   f) caudal peduncle   g) anal fin   h) pectoral fin
i) pelvic fin   j) operculum   k) mouth

BODY SHAPES

BARRACUDA

GROUPER

CORAL TROUT

SWEETLIPS

SNAPPER

PARROTFISH

TRIGGERFISH

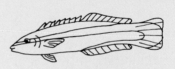

CLEANER WRASSE

PUFFERFISH

PORCUPINEFISH

BOXFISH

TRUMPETFISH

GOBY

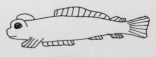

BLENNY

OF REEF FISH

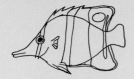

BUTTERFLYFISH

ANGELFISH

SURGEONFISH

MOORISH IDOL

RABBITFISH

DAMSELFISH

BATFISH

GOATFISH

SQUIRRELFISH

LIZARDFISH

MORAY EELS

ANEMONEFISH

SCORPIONFISH

LIONFISH

Barracuda (*Sphyraena sp.*)
Shoals of juvenile barracuda have a habit of encircling
divers and eyeing them with curious intent. Nevertheless,
these young specimens usually keep their distance!

Barracuda (*Sphyraena sp.*)

Barracuda have all of the characteristics of a typical bony fish as
well as some specialised features that equip them for effective pre-
dation. Their body is streamlined for rapid movement, while their
jaws are large and equipped with powerful fang-like teeth.

Barracuda start their lives in large shoals. As time goes by, the
individual members of these shoals become steadily larger in size and
fewer in number. Sometimes shoals of what look like 'ikan bilis' are
actually barracuda fingerlings. Shoals of maturing barracuda are
often seen at locations like Tokong Bahara and Labas off the East
Coast of Malaysia. By the time barracudas mature to a length of
two metres or longer, they are usually paired or solitary.

Barracuda (*Sphyraena sp.*)
Although awesome in
appearance with their protruding jaws and fierce-
looking teeth, barracudas
in the Indo-Pacific are not
normally dangerous to
divers. In fact, they pose a
more serious threat from
being eaten. It is not widely
known that barracuda flesh
can be subject to ciguatera
poisoning.

Barracudas feed by sight and attack when they see erratic movement or violent flashing of a wounded fish. Generally, barracudas do not threaten divers. In fact, quite the contrary is true – the large ones keep their distance and decline to be photographed at close range!

Grouper (*Epinephelus sp.*)

Grouper are also known as rock cod and are a favourite delicacy of local cuisines. Mature adults reach a considerable size, but smaller or medium-sized specimens are favoured for eating.

Grouper vary tremendously in colour. The grey type with darker spots is generally the most common. When in danger, groupers exhibit a bicolour effect, turning light underneath and dark on their upper or dorsal surface.

The grouper's daytime haunt is beneath ledges or in caves. Its usual sluggish movement is achieved by alternate movements of the pectoral fins. When a more rapid movement is needed (such as when the grouper attacks its prey), the powerful back muscles are brought into action. The tail fin then launches the fish into action at remarkable speed.

Grouper (*Epinephelus sp.*)
Meeting a full-sized grouper face to face under-water could be a disconcerting experience. Groupers are harmless, however, and if they encounter a natural enemy, they prefer to retreat to the protection of caves.

Coral Trout (*Cephalopholis miniatus*)
Coral trout live in crevices or small caves and move lethargically.
When feeding, they position themselves among the branches of
staghorn corals to wait for smaller fish such as damsels to venture
within striking distance.

Coral Trout (*Cephalopholis miniatus*)

A close relative of the grouper, the coral trout is smaller and
more colourful. Members of this genus vary greatly in colour, but
the deep red variety with iridescent green spots is commonly seen
in the Indo-Pacific.

Although coral trout feed on other fish, they are not aggressive
and they feed with minimum effort. In fact, they prefer to lurk
around the branches of staghorn coral waiting for an unsuspecting
damsel fish to pass close to them before bothering to attack.

Coral trout, like groupers, also undergo interesting changes during their sexual development. They first mature as females and produce eggs. As they grow larger, they change sex and become func-
tioning males.

Many-spotted Sweetlips (*Plectorhyncus chaetodontoides*)

The common name of this species of sweetlips is an accurate
description of its markings. Spots cover all but the underpart of the
body and some of the spots are distinctly hexagonal in shape.

The many-spotted sweetlips can reach one metre in length as adults
and can be seen by day in the lee of large coral heads.

The several species of sweetlips are relatives of the snappers. Their
obvious identifiable feature is the thick fleshy lips after which all
members of the group are named.

**Many-spotted Sweetlips
(*Plectorhyncus sp.*)**
Although protected by an overhang,
the thick fleshy lips and dark markings
(some of which are hexagonal) of this
spotted sweetlips reveal its identity.

Parrotfish (*Scarus sp.*)

Parrotfish are among the most brilliantly hued fish found on the reef. They can be seen in shallow areas 'pecking' at corals or feeding on sea urchins they have attacked or those that have fallen victim to other predators.

Parrotfish can grow up to 70 cm in length. In most species, males, females and juveniles are differently coloured. The rainbow parrot fish and the blue parrot fish are the most common types found in the South China Sea.

The beak-like mouth is made up of fused teeth which are effective in scraping algae from rocks and corals. While feeding, parrotfish rasp away chunks of coral containing live polyps and they pulverise this mixture using special grinders in their throat. After ingesting the living portion of the coral, they spit out the hard parts in the form of fine sand.

Parrotfish also have an unusual nocturnal habit of secreting a protective mucous cocoon around themselves. This cocoon can take up to 30 minutes to secrete and it is believed to act as a barrier to prevent nocturnal predators from detecting their presence.

Parrotfish (*Scarus sp.*)
Parrotfish are among the most common fish found on the reef, but because of
the great variety of these fish in the Indo-Pacific region, identification of species
is far from easy. The fact that juvenile forms are often differently coloured from
adults makes identification even more difficult.

Blue Parrotfish
(*Scarus sp.*)
Sleeping in a crevice surrounded by its mucous cocoon, this blue parrotfish is securely settled for the night. As active daytime feeders, they can be seen feeding on algae or nibbling at coral polyps during the day. It is believed that the mucous cocoon produced by parrotfish at night is to mask their scent from predators.

Bump-head Parrotfish
(*Scarus sp.*)
The beak-like jaws of parrotfish are the result of fused teeth on the upper and lower jaws. Such a beak is an ideal tool to scrape away coral polyps. This bump-head parrotfish is showing off its dentition to full effect!

Picasso Triggerfish (*Rhinecanthus aculeatus*)

The common name of 'triggerfish' is shared by the Picasso triggerfish and other similarly shaped fish due to the modified dorsal fin that forms a stiff spike somewhat like a trigger. When escaping marauding predators, triggerfish dart into small crevices and erect their trigger-like dorsal fin which locks or 'triggers' into place, ensuring that the fish cannot be dislodged. In some triggerfish, a modified ventral fin works in conjunction with the dorsal fin.

Compared with other triggerfish, the Picasso triggerfish is relatively small, reaching only about 30 cm in length. Nevertheless, its powerful jaws enable it to effectively prey on crabs, prawns and small molluscs.

Found throughout the Indo-Pacific region, the Picasso triggerfish is also common around the Hawaiian island chain where it is known as the lagoon triggerfish. Its Hawaiian name, 'Humuhumu-nukunuku-a-pua'a', refers to its needle-like spines and its habit of grunting loudly if disturbed. When translated into English its Hawaiian name means: 'the fish that sews and grunts like a pig'.

Picasso Triggerfish (*Rhinecanthus aculeatus*)
The Picasso triggerfish is smaller and less colourful than some of its relatives. It will make a peculiar grunting noise if harassed.

Pink-tail Triggerfish (*Melichthys vidua*)
The pink-tail triggerfish is usually seen in deeper areas of the coral reef. The pectoral fins are yellow and the dorsal and anal fins are pale with dark markings. Normally, the triggerfish glides along using the anal and dorsal fins, but when a quick burst of speed is necessary, they use their entire body.

Scribbled Leatherjacket (*Aluterus scriptus*)
With unmistakable blue scribbled markings and black spots, the scribbled leatherjacket is an impressive fish. Its body is compressed laterally and its snout and tail are almost mirror images of each other, both being long and pointed. Scribbled leatherjackets can reach a length of one metre.

Lyretail Wrasse (*Thalasomma lunare*)

Also called the moon wrasse, this attractive reef fish resembles the parrot fish in its basic colouration. The adults are bright blue-green with striking pink bands radiating from the eye. The same pink colour borders the tail fin which, as its name suggests, resembles the shape of a moon or lyre instrument. A similar wrasse (*Halichoeres sp.*) is common in Singapore waters except that this species has blue lines radiating from the eye and bordering the tail fin. Both species reach a maximum size of 30 cm.

Wrasses have a curious mode of swimming. Under normal conditions these fish move slowly, apparently propelling themselves by use of only the pectoral fins. If they are alarmed, however, the fish will engage in short bursts of speed which are unequalled in any other coral fish. Wrasses are essentially carnivorous feeders, feeding on small shrimp, crab or shellfish.

Lyretail Wrasse (*Thalasomma lunare*)
Divers who pick up or turn over rocks will notice the almost instant appearance of a couple of lyretail wrasses. They are relentless opportunitic scavengers.

Bird Wrasse (*Gomphosus varius*)

The bird wrasse is aptly named because: 1) its head is very definitely bird-like with elongated, beak-shaped jaws, and 2) its mode of swimming by propelling itself with its pectoral fins causes it to flit through the water at remarkable speed, somewhat resembling a bird in flight.

Males and females can easily be distinguished from each other. While the female is brown in colour, the male is larger, has a blue beak and head, and its predominantly greenish body blends into a blue peduncle and tail. A brighter yellow-green blotch visible above the peduncle is also an indicator that the specimen is a male.

Bird wrasses are carnivorous and feed mainly on crustaceans. They can sometimes be seen swimming with other wrasses as they feed. Females are also quite often seen swimming in small groups.

Bird Wrasse (male) (*Gomphosus varius*)
The bird wrasse is an active fish that moves at great speed by sculling through the water with its pectoral fins. It acquired its common name because of its bird-like movements and its elongated jaws which resemble a beak.

Bird Wrasse (female) (*Gomphosus varius*)
Less colourful and slightly smaller than their male counterparts, female bird wrasse exhibit the same type of 'flitting' movement. Females are sometimes seen swimming in small groups.

Thick-lipped Wrasse (*Hemigymnus melapterus*)
This large edible wrasse can reach up to one metre in length. The anterior portion of its body is light in colour and delicately lined. The scales of the body of the fish are distinctly marked. The dorsal fin has 9–10 spines and 10–11 rays. The most distinctive feature of this wrasse is, of course, the thick bony lips.

Thick-lipped Wrasse (*Hemigymnus melapterus*)
Several types of fish have what is referred to an an extensible mouth. When extended, a bony, plated tube protudes forward, greatly extanding the distance from which prey can be captured.

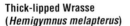

Giant Maori Wrasse (*Cheilinus sp.*)
The giant Maori wrasse is notable for its non-descript grey colour and the large bump on its head. The unusually large scales are typical of this giant-sized wrasse.

Speckled Wrasse (*Anampses sp.*)
This attractive wrasse can be found in waters from the Indo-Pacific to Polynesia. It is distinguished from a similar Hawaiian species by the blue ringed black oscellus on the dorsal and anal rays.

Emperor Snapper (*Lutjanus sabae*)
This splendid fish is now rather rare on accessible reefs. Its body is deep with three broad red bands. The margins of the dorsal and anal fins are a blackish colour. The contrasting bands evident in this juvenile become less distinct as the fish matures. The adult form is therefore more or less a uniform red colour. The emperor snapper can grow up to one metre in length.

White Spotted Pufferfish (*Arothron hispidus*)
Pufferfish, such as the white spotted puffer, are omnivorous and eat a variety of algae, crustaceans, molluscs and echinoderms. Note the distinctive teeth in the centre of the lower jaws and the large nostrils which are positioned high up on the snout, just below the eyes.

White Spotted Pufferfish (*Arothron hispidus*)

The spotted pufferfish is one of the larger species of pufferfish which sometimes (but rarely) reaches a maximum length of one metre. Pufferfish are slow moving but they have developed special ways of protecting themselves against their enemies. They are able to inflate a series of sacs that line the intestine, thus drastically increasing their size. Alternatively, they can bury themselves in the sand by squirming around on the sea bed.

Pufferfish are omnivorous in their feeding habits. Among their sources of food are algae, echinoderms, worms, molluscs, crustaceans and ascidians. In some species their teeth are fused to form a hard, parrot-like beak. When not feeding, puffers might be found resting on a ledge or in a cave with their tail curved around their body.

Although the skin and internal organs of all pufferfish are extremely toxic, their flesh is considered a delicacy in some countries. Specially trained Japanese chefs prepare a dish called 'fugu' from the dissected flesh of the puffer. But despite the precautions taken in the preparation of this dish, a few unlucky gourmets die each year from pufferfish poisoning.

Masked Pufferfish (*Arothron sp.*)
The grey colouring, black fins and black patches over the eyes and around the mouth are the distinctive features of this pufferfish. Tiny black flaps are also present over the nostrils.

Guinea Fowl Pufferfish (*Arothron meleagris*)
During the day time, puffers may be found resting inside caves or on ledges with their tail curled alongside their body.

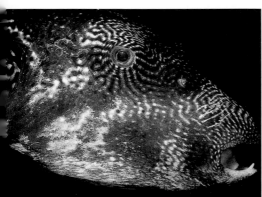

Starry Pufferfish (*Arothron stellatus*)
Starry pufferfish are among the largest of the puffers and, in some parts of the Indo-Pacific, can approach one metre in length. Their body is covered with small spines and corresponding black dots which are larger at the base of the fins. The flesh is edible but the viscera and skin are extremely poisonous.

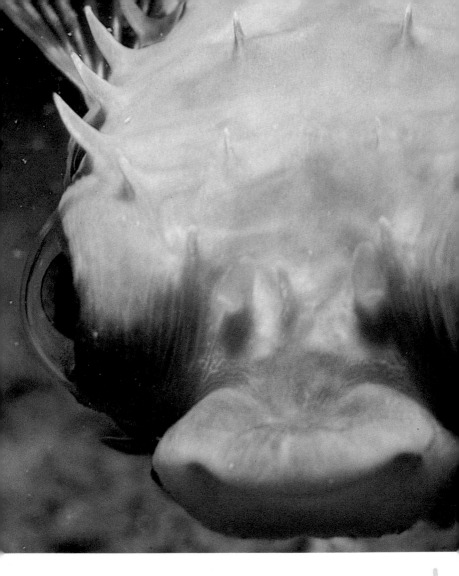

Freckled Porcupinefish (*Diodon sp.*)

Porcupinefish belong to the family Diodontidae which means 'two teeth'. This characteristic distinguishes porcupinefish from puffers and blowfish which have a different dentition altogether.

Like pufferfish, porcupinefish have a defence mechanism which enable them to imbibe huge amounts of water and increase their size enormously. In this distended condition the spines that normally lie flat against the body stand out at an angle and the porcupinefish looks rather like a spiky ball with the face of a Pekinese dog.

If alarmed, a partly inflated porcupinefish may rise to the surface and inadvertently take in air instead of water. Under these circumstances, it may become impossible for them to later release the air and they risk floating around on the surface until they perish.

Young Freckled Porcupinefish (*Diodon holocanthus*)
The bulging eyes and enlarged lips of this young freckled porcupinefish are accentuated because it has been photographed in a normal, uninflated state. The thick lips enclose powerful jaws which are able to crush the hard body parts of the molluscs and crustaceans on which it preys.

Freckled Porcupinefish (*Diodon holocanthus*)
Porcupinefish flesh and liver is 500 times as toxic as cyanide. It is apparently the vital ingredient in the 'coup poudre' used by Haitian voodoo believers to kill or reduce their enemies to zombies.

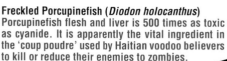

Boxfish (*Ostracion sp.*)
The boxfish does indeed resemble a box. The scales have been fused to form a solid box with openings for the eyes, mouth and tail.

Boxfish (*Ostracion sp.*)

The common name of 'boxfish' aptly describes the atypical appearance of this fish. Boxfish do indeed resemble a bony box with a mouth, eyes and fins.

The movement of boxfish is fascinating to watch. Because their body is so rigid, they can only propel themselves by means of their pectoral, pelvic and tail fins. Nevertheless, boxfish have great manoeuvrability. If you approach them too closely, they will turn promptly on their horizontal axis and retreat hurriedly to shelter.

Boxfish have a unique defence mechanism – their skin has specialised structures which can secrete a very powerful poison into the water. The poison has no effect on the boxfish itself.

Juvenile forms of *Ostracion* have a different colouration altogether, bright yellow with small, dark spots.

Painted Flutemouth (*Aulostomus chinensis*)

The painted flutemouth is one of a group of fish also known as trumpetfish. All members of the group have similar body characteristics. Their sleek, pipe-like body presents an unusual contour against the uneven colours and shapes of the reef. *Aulostomus* can reach 75 cm in length and has powerful, elongated jaws. The aptly-named painted flutemouth has three different colour phases: yellow, greyish-blue with white markings, and red with black and white markings.

The flutemouth is a diurnal predator. Its method of hunting is an intriguing form of behavioural adaptation. Often the flutemouth will use other fish for cover as it approaches schools of small fish such as damsels. Generally, the cover will be a herbivore or larger predator that usually does not prey on the types of fish the flutemouth is stalking. So skilled is the flutemouth in using other fish in this manner, it will even select a fish of a similar colour, ie. the yellow phase will choose a yellow fish whilst the later phases will select a fish of a compatible hue.

Painted Flutemouth (*Aulostomus chinensis*)
The painted flutemouth or trumpetfish is a skilled predator. It will use other fish for cover as it stalks its prey. In selecting larger fish that are not normally threatening to the fish it is stalking, the flutefish maximises its opportunity for success in capturing its prey.

Mesoleucus Angelfish (*Chaetodontoplus mesoleucus*)

Also called the Singapore angelfish, this species is the most common angelfish seen in Singapore and Malaysian waters. It reaches a length of 20 cm and can be identified by its blue lips and the broad black stripe that runs vertically through the eye. Its black dorsal fin and peduncle is a sharp contrast to its bright yellow tail.

The Mesoleucus angelfish is small compared to other angelfish and it is solitary in its habits. Unlike most other angelfish of the Indo-Pacific region, it is not territorial and can be seen feeding during the daytime anywhere on the reef slope.

Six-banded Angelfish (*Euxiphipops sextriatus*)

The six-banded angelfish is a fairly large and common angelfish in Singapore and Malaysian waters. It can reach a maximum length of 50 cm. Its basic colour is a yellow or beige-brown and each scale is marked with a bright blue spot. The anal fin and tail are spotted and edged with the same iridescent blue colour. A vertical white stripe behind the eye divides the head into two sections.

Six-banded angelfish are frequently seen in pairs roaming the reef, but they will make for the cover of an overhang or cave if approached. They range from a depth of 5 to 25 metres and seem to prefer more open, rocky areas of the reef when they feed.

Mesoleucus Angelfish (*Chaetodontoplus mesoleucus*)
By far the most common angelfish in Singapore waters, the Mesoleucus angelfish is also known as the Singapore Angelfish, the yellow-tailed angelfish or the vermiculated angelfish. The most prominent marking of this angelfish is the dark stripe which passes through the eye. Such markings are common in both angelfish and butterflyfish. They are intended to camouflage the eye and also to confuse predators.

The Six-banded Angelfish (*Euxiphipops sextriatus*)
The six-banded angelfish can be identified by six dark vertical stripes on its body. A distinctive white stripe lies behind the eye while the dorsal and anal fins are spotted.

Regal Angelfish (*Pygoplytes diacanthus*)
The regal angelfish is a beautifully coloured but shy fish that is difficult to approach. Regals are territorial and although sometimes seen in pairs, they are mostly solitary in habit. Regal angelfish swim actively, feeding on encrusting organisms.

Regal Angelfish (*Pygoplites diacanthus*)

This beautifully marked angelfish is occasionally seen at dive sites either as solitary individuals or in pairs. Each crescent-shaped band on its body is elegantly outlined in black and merges into striations on the dorsal and anal fins. Regals can reach a maximum length of 20 cm.

The favourite territory of the regal angelfish is at the reef drop-off at around 10-25 metres where they can be seen feeding by day. They graze on encrusting sessile organisms and algae that grow on rocks or cave underhangings.

Like many other species of angelfish, the regal angelfish is territorial in habit, occupying the same caves or ledges over a period of time.

Emperor Angelfish (*Pomacanthus imperator*)

The adult emperor angelfish is surely one of the most spectacular if rare sights on accessible reefs. Its horizontal blue-purple and bright yellow stripes merge into an orange-coloured tail. Also distinctive is the black curved stripe that creates what looks like a mask covering the eyes.

An adult emperor angel can reach a size of at least 30 cm. The young are generally dark blue and marked with a series of concentric white rings. The spine projecting downwards from the gill cover is a characteristic feature of angelfish.

When disturbed, the emperor angelfish will utter a curious clicking sound that can be clearly heard under water.

Emperor Angelfish (*Pomocanthus imperator*)
The emperor angelfish is a spectacular fish, impressive not only because of its splendid colouration and markings, but also because of its size. An adult emperor angelfish can reach a length of 30 cm.

Yellow-faced Angelfish (*Euxiphipops xanthometapon*)

The yellow-faced angel is yet another vividly coloured and beautifully marked angelfish. While most of the head is marked with blue, the eyes are connected with a yellow mask. Each scale is bordered with gold and the fins are outlined in blue.

One of the larger species of angelfish, the adult yellow-faced angel can reach 35 cm in length. This species is very elusive. On the rare occasions when it is sighted, it will retreat into caves or under ledges.

Euxiphipops feeds on encrusting sessile organisms. It seems to prefer areas where there is a lot of water movement, such as in channels around offshore reefs.

Yellow-faced Angelfish (*Euxiphipops xanthometapon*)
Some might consider the yellow-faced angelfish gaudy in appearance. It is certainly more vividly coloured than many other angelfish. It is also very elusive in nature, retreating to the cover of caves and ledges when divers are around.

Blue-ring Angelfish (*Pomacanthus annularis*)

Pomacanthus annularis is one of the more common angelfish on Malaysian reefs. Its common name is blue-ring angelfish due to the curved blue markings and the blue ring near the eye, it is also called the blue-king angelfish.

The blue-ring angel feeds by day on encrusting sessile organisms such as sponges, ascidians, and algae. Its brush-like teeth are well equipped for the necessary scraping action. Both juveniles and adults are equally shy and difficult to approach.

As in many other reef species, the colouration and markings of the juvenile blue-ring is markedly different from the adults.

**Blue-ring Angelfish
(*Pomacanthus annularis*)**
The blue-ring angelfish is often seen in caves in pairs. Like many species of angelfish, they are territorial in habit and they curiously inspect anything that enters their territory.

Semicircle Angelfish (*Pomacanthus semicirculatus*)

The semicircle angelfish is sometimes called the Koran angelfish due to the pattern formed by the blue markings on the tail of the juvenile form. These markings are thought to resemble verses from the Koran and, for this reason, the fish is much revered. In common with other angelfish, the semicircle angelfish is very territorial and mated pairs are often seen patrolling low shallow caves. The synchronised back-and-forth movement they exhibit inside the cave is due to a type of aggressive response to the body patterning of their own species.

The differentiated body pattern of juvenile semicircle angels enables them to avoid attack by their own species until they are mature enough to establish their own territory. This is true for several species of angelfish.

Semicircle Angelfish (*Pomacanthus semicirculatus*) Pairs of semicircle angelfish are often seen patrolling low, shallow caves. This back and forth movement is reported to be an aggressive response to the markings of members of its own species. The juvenile form of the semicircle angelfish has a different colouration and is sometimes mistaken for a different species altogether.

Juvenile Semicircle Angelfish (*Pomacanthus semicirculatus*) This juvenile is in the process of changing to an adult. Already the dorsal and anal fins are edged with blue, as is the tail fin. The different colouration of juveniles confuses predators. Protection is therefore afforded when it is most needed.

Three-spot Angelfish (*Holacanthus trimaculatus*)
The common name of this handsome angelfish is derived from three black spots
(a single spot on the forehead and two spots behind both eyes). The broad black
band bordering the anal fin is also a helpful identifying feature.

White-cheeked Surgeonfish (*Acanthurus glaucopareius*)
Surgeonfish are so-called because of the sharp blade-like spine which is located on either side of the caudal peduncle. Normally the spines lie flat, but they become erect when the fish is disturbed, enabling it to inflict severe injuries on the offending predator.

White-cheeked Surgeonfish (*Acanthurus glaucopareius*)

Surgeonfish get their name from the sharp knife-like spine located on either side of the caudal peduncle. Normally, the spines are located in a groove lying flat against the body. When the fish is disturbed, the spines will become erect and can be used to inflict severe wounds on the intruder.

As one of the hundred or so species of surgeonfish, the white-cheeked surgeonfish can be identified by the yellow lines which follow the contour of the body and the white markings on the snout and under the eye. The adult size is around 25 cm.

The white-cheeked surgeon is solitary and territorial. It is often found atop coral heads where there is a profusion of coral growth and the current is quite strong. They are active feeders and their diet is mainly encrusting algae.

**Blue Surgeonfish
(*Paracanthurus hepatus*)**
Blue surgeonfish are widely distributed in the Indo-Pacific and can be found from East Africa to the Philippines. The blue surgeonfish is striking in colour and markings. The yellow tail contrasts sharply with the predominantly blue and black-streaked body.

Powder-blue Surgeonfish
(*Acanthurus leucosternon*)
Fairly common throughout some areas of the Indo-Pacific, the powder-blue surgeonfish is a prize aquarium fish. Its attractive appearance may well be a deciding factor in the future of the powder-blue in its natural habitat. The powder-blue is relatively large, sometimes reaching 30 cm in length.

Powder-blue Surgeonfish (*Acanthurus leucosternon*)

The uncommon but beautiful powder-blue surgeonfish is a uniform turquoise blue with a black face, a prominent yellow dorsal fin and a white 'chin-strap' which extends from beneath the lower jaw to the pectoral fin. The powder-blue can reach 30 cm in length and is larger than most other surgeonfish.

Surgeonfish are also commonly referred to as 'tangs'. Their characteristic oval-shaped body is a result of the dorsal and anal fins being almost the same shape.

Smooth-head Unicornfish (*Naso lituratus*)
Related to the surgeonfish are the unicornfish. This species of unicornfish inhabits shallow areas of the coral reef. It is edible and reaches about 60 cm in length.

Moorish Idol (*Zanclus canescens*)

Moorish idols are the only representative of their family Zanclidae. They are related to surgeonfish, even though their body shape is quite different. Reaching a maximum size of 20 cm, Moorish idols feed carnivorously on encrusting sessile invertebrates such as sponges.

Moorish idols can be seen moving around the reef as individuals, in pairs, or in large groups. It is believed that they congregate in large groups prior to spawning.

The elongated snout of Moorish idols is marked with a yellow or copper saddle and, when their mouths are open, their thick lips protrude outwards in a characteristic 'pout'.

Moorish Idol (*Zanclus canescens*)
The Moorish idol has elongated jaws, 'pouting' lips and the saddle marking across the snout. This fish is splendid in appearance and graceful in its movements. Moorish idols should not be confused with bannerfish which have a much shorter snout and a less impressive pennant fin.

**Fox-faced Rabbitfish
(*Siganus vulpinus*)**
The spines in the dorsal fin of rabbitfish are poisonous. The wound inflicted by these spines is extremely painful and slow to heal. The fox-face rabbitfish will change colour completely to a dull brown if unduly disturbed.

Fox-face Rabbitfish (*Siganus vulpinus*)

Like the Moorish idol, the rabbitfish is often seen in pairs but it is much more retiring in nature, preferring to remain close to sheltered reef crevices.

Rabbitfish feed on algae and other sessile organisms and they cover large areas of the reef in search of food. The fox-face rabbitfish is relatively large (20 cm as an adult) and brilliantly coloured. Its yellow body and velvet black-and-white-striped face make it one of the reef's most striking fish. Rabbitfish are also among the more dangerous reef inhabitants as their dorsal spines are highly venomous.

One of the curious features of the rabbitfish is that every eight to ten days it sheds its mucous covering and immediately replenishes it by secreting another.

Siganus vulpinus is alternatively classified under a different genus – 'Lo' – which is the Samoan vernacular name for rabbitfish.

**Spotted Rabbitfish
(*Siganus sp.*)**
The rationale behind its common name is clearly seen in the rounded head and rabbit-like mouth. Like their namesake, rabbitfish are grazers feeding on algae and other marine plants in shallow inshore waters. This species drastically changes colour at night.

Teira Batfish (*Platax teira*)

Batfish is a popular common name given to a number of fish that have certain features in common: a fan-shaped body, dorsal and anal fins that are grossly enlarged and dark vertical stripes, one of which passes through the eye. The teira batfish can be distinguished from other species by its yellow pectoral fins.

The diet and feeding habits of the teira batfish appear to be very varied. They can sometimes be seen out on the reef feeding on filamentous algae during the early morning. Alternatively, under other conditions, they may feed on sea jellies and planktonic ascidians at the fringe of the reef.

Batfish are often seen in groups and are clearly territorial. They consistently occupy selected areas of the reef for a period of time.

Teira Batfish (*Platax teira*)
Distinguishable from other batfish by its yellow pectoral fins, the teira batfish can sometimes be seen swimming in large schools over wrecks and coral heads. Batfish are inquisitive fish, prone to following divers over some distance.

Batfish (*Platax sp.*)
Batfish are large fish compared to other reef fishes. Their body is flattened laterally and, in the adult form, they are fanshaped and silvery-white in colour. Batfish undergo dramatic transformations from the juvenile form to adulthood and it is often difficult to identify the exact species. Adult forms of most species lose the vertical black bars around the eyes and their fins take on a less triangular shape.

Pinnate Batfish (*Platax pinnatus*)
This juvenile form of the pinnate batfish, also known as the orange-ring or long-finned batfish, has dorsal and anal fins with orange borders. The body is leaf-shaped due to the enlarged fins. The juvenile is much darker than the adult. Juvenile forms sometimes drift on their sides, mimicking certain unpalatable flatworms, thus avoiding predators.

Pinnate Batfish (*Platax pinnatus*)
In the transitional stage, the dorsal and anal fins of the pinnate batfish are much reduced and the body is lighter in colour. The adult form of *Platax pinnatus* is distinguished by its slightly projecting snout.

Copperband Butterflyfish
(*Chelmon rostratus*)
Butterflyfish are so-called because their erratic movement during feeding is reminiscent of the movement of a butterfly. The copperband butterfly is a particularly beautiful species with alternating orange and silver stripes that have a metallic lustre. The dark spot on the dorsal fin is the oscellus.

Copperband Butterflyfish (*Chelmon rostratus*)

Called the long-nosed butterfly or the beaked coralfish in some countries, the copperband may often be seen in pairs, in shallow areas of the reef. Copperbands use their elongated jaws and small mouths almost like precision surgical instruments to poke into rock crevices and feed on small sessile invertebrates.

The laterally flattened body of the copperband is striped with combinations of black, silver and orange. Many butterflyfish are striped in this manner. Characteristically, one of the stripes passes through the eye. This furnishes a disguise for this very vulnerable part of the body.

The large black spot (called an oscellus) on the caudal fin of the copperband is sometimes referred to as a 'false eye'. This is believed to be a protective device designed to fool predators as to which direction the fish is likely to move in the event of a hurried escape.

Meyer's Butterflyfish (*Chaetodon meyeri*)

The adult butterflyfish reaches a size of around 20 cm. It is carnivorous, feeding on coral polyps on the outer reef faces and drop-offs. It is seen only infrequently and it is difficult to approach.

Meyer's butterflyfish has an extremely specialised diet, selecting only certain corals to prey upon. This type of selective feeding leads to favourable cropping of the reef by the fish population. It is beneficial not only in reducing competition for food among fish, but it may also help to maintain a balance of coral species that make up the reef.

Meyer's Butterflyfish
(*Chaetodon meyeri*)
Unlike some of its relatives, the rare Meyer's butterflyfish is a solitary creature that frequents outer reef drop-offs at 10–15 metres. It is a retiring species that is difficult to approach and even more difficult to photograph.

Baronessa Butterflyfish (*Chaetodon baronessa*)

Feeding selectively on staghorn corals, the baronessa butterflyfish is usually seen in pairs in shallow, sheltered areas of the reef around bommies or on the reef slope.

The adult size is 15 cm and the overall shape of the fish is typical of butterflyfish. The baronessa is elusive and difficult to approach. It is an active feeder and continuously on the move.

Baronessa Butterflyfish (*Chaetodon baronessa*)
Two distinguishing features of the baronessa butterflyfish are the pointed, reddish snout and well-developed, almost symmetrical dorsal and anal fins.

Eight-banded Butterflyfish (*Chaetodon octofasciatus*)
Less brilliantly coloured than many of its relatives, the eight-banded butterflyfish does indeed have eight vertical stripes marking its body.

Bantayan Butterflyfish (*Chaetodon adiergastos*)
Quite common in Indo-Pacific waters, the Bantayan butterflyfish is usually seen in pairs. It can be identified by the broad blotch over the eye and the smaller dot on the head.

BOTTOM DWELLERS

Fish that are associated with the ocean floor are referred to as 'bottom dwellers'. Bottom dwellers either feed among the debris on the ocean floor, as is the case of the goatfish, or they are so well camouflaged they can remain undetected in a stationary position for long periods of time (such as the lizardfish, the gobies, the scorpionfish and the stonefishes).

Bottom dwellers demonstrate a set of common adaptations like eyes that are raised above the level of the head, a body that is 'bottom heavy' (wider on the ventral than on the dorsal surface) and powerful jaws that enable them to seize choice prey. Some bottom dwellers partially bury themselves in the sand while others prop themselves up on their pectoral fins.

Common Goatfish (*Mulloidichthys sp.*)
The common goatfish is mottled and well camouflaged, with a prominent red lateral stripe. The most distinctive feature of all goatfish is the pair of 'whiskers' or barbels which they use to probe the sand for food.

Freckled Goby
(*Chasmichthys sp.*)
Many types of gobies live on the reef and all are bottom dwellers. Their large protruding eyes peer inquisitively at close range. Some gobies are very brightly coloured and quick to dart to safety.

Lizardfish (*Synodus sp.*)
Quite commonly seen propped up by its pectoral fins awaiting unsuspecting prey, the lizardfish has a decidedly reptilian appearance. Lizardfish are well camouflaged and may be seen in pairs, motionless in the sand or on a rock.

Lizardfish (*Synodus sp.*)

This common fish is notable for its habit of remaining stationary, either partly buried in the sand or perched on a ledge, propped up by its pectoral fins. Its superb camouflage enables it to lie discretely awaiting unsuspecting prey. When suitably sized small fish come within reach, the lizardfish will rapidly spring into action and seize its prey in its sizable jaws.

Lizardfish do not have a swim bladder or organ that helps most bony fish to maintain neutral buoyancy. As in most bottom dwellers, the swim bladder of *Synodus* has degenerated over the course of evolution as it was not required for their way of life. Because of the absence of the swim bladder, lizardfish sink to the bottom if they are not swimming and they remain in a motionless resting postion most of the time.

The reason for the lizardfish's name is obvious. The shape of its head, its protruding eyes and rounded jaws are reptilian in appearance. Its pose as it waits to capture its prey is also reminiscent of a lizard sunning itself on a rock.

Scorpionfish (*Scorpaenopsis sp.*)
The colour of scorpionfish varies according to their habitat. The organisms that colonise the scorpionfish's warty skin add further camouflage. The result is that the scorpionfish is virtually undetectable when it is ensconced among rocks and coral rubble that is colonised by similar organisms.

Stonefish (*Synanceia horrida*)
With their stubby, bottom-heavy body, stonefish are the most grotesque and dreaded of all fish. Their pitted, warty skin is colonised by algae and other organisms giving them near perfect camouflage as they lie nestled among rocks and coral debris.

CAVE DWELLERS

Among the rocks and coral formations to be found on a coral reef, caves of different sizes and forms provide a habitat for a variety of reef inhabitants. Few remain permanently in their cave as many of them are nocturnal and may be found in open water at night. Red is a common colour for cave dwellers because red appears black in the reduced light conditions of the cave.

Squirrelfish (*Sargocentron sp.*)

Squirrelfish are cave-dwelling, nocturnal fish, so called because of their large squirrel-like eyes. At night when they are most active they can be seen foraging for food in groups of 6-20 individuals. Squirrelfish commonly feed around coral heads on the reef slope. Their large glassy eyes are a good indicator of their noctural habits.

Squirrelfish have very spiny dorsal fins. They also have a spine on their cheeks and anal fins. Squirrelfish tend to stay in one main area as adults but the juveniles are dispersed long distances by the current.

Bigeye Soldierfish (*Myripristis sp.*)

Often confused with squirrelfish, bigeyes have several distinctive features. Their large eye is the most obvious feature but their body shape is rounder and bulkier and more evenly coloured than most squirrelfish. The leading edge of their polvic, dorsal and anal fins are edged with white and they lack the spine on the preoperculum.

Squirrelfish (*Adioryx sp.*)

Squirrelfish are found in groups of seven to ten. They spend most of the daytime in caves. Many species are striped. The snout is long and the gill cover bears several spines, the longest of which is on the preoperculum.

Long-jawed Squirrelfish (*Adioryx spinifer*)

Often reaching a length of 45 cm, the long-jawed squirrelfish is larger than most other species. It also lacks the stripes characteristic of most squirrelfish. Its brilliant orange red colour and the white stripes that mark the contours of the head make it a remarkably handsome species.

MORAY EELS

Because of the retiring nature of the moray eel and its tendency to feed by night, there are probably more morays on the reef than is immediately apparent. Their daytime haunts are small caves or crevices which they often share with cleaner shrimp. The cleaner shrimp groom the moray's smooth scaleless skin by feeding on parasites, thus relieving it from damaging infestations. In turn, the shrimps benefit by being protected from attack by predators such as the wrasses.

If morays are seen during the day, there is generally little more than a head, two menacingly beady eyes and a pair of lethal looking jaws poking out of their retreat. Actually, the vicious appearance of the moray is deceptive. It is a relatively retiring creature which only gapes its jaws to facilitate breathing.

Divers who feed morays will notice that they are immediately attracted to the scent of dead or injured fish.

Net Moray Eel (*Gymnothorax reticularis*)
A small species which inhabits deeper waters, the net moray can reach 60 cm in length and can be identified by its 14–20 darker cross bands. It is pictured here on a night feeding foray.

Moray Eel (*Gymnothorax sp.*)
Being a very ancient form of fish, morays lack fins and scales. During the day they anchor the rear portion of their body in a coral crevice which they have selected as their retreat. The giant moray is one of the largest morays. Its body is thick, its head large, and its snout thick and short.

Moray Eel (*Gymnothorax sp.*)
There is little chance of being bitten by a moray unless you reach into a crevice without first looking to see what is there. Morays feed mainly by smell and will be attracted to dead or injured fish. Like barracudas, they are also attracted to shiny, fast-moving objects.

Moray Eel (*Gymnothorax sp.*)
Less frequently seen than other moray eels, this species has elongated jaws and long sharp teeth. This specimen is in a characteristic moray 'pose' with mouth agape and nostrils flaring.

111

FISH THAT SCHOOL

Fishes of all sizes and shapes form schools. Schooling is an adaptive behaviour. The most obvious benefit is that it confuses predators. Schools with a large number of members fill the visual field of predators making it difficult for them to target on one individual for attack. In other species, be they grazers or carnivores, schooling makes searching for food a more efficient process.

Yellowtail Jacks

Pennant Coralfish (*Heniochus acuminatus*)
Often confused with the Moorish Idol, the pennant coralfish are also known as bannerfish. The pennant is actually an extension of the fourth spine of the dorsal fin. Juveniles have a shorter pennant but identical markings. Pennant coralfish are omnivorous feeders.

Razorfish (*Aeliscus strigatus*)
These curious fish swim in a vertical fashion with their heads pointed down-wards. They feed on small crustaceans which they probe out of the coral or snap up as they pass in the current. Razorfish may be found in small schools.

Fusilierfish (*Paracaesio sp.*)

Fusiliers swim at the edges of the reef in large schools where they continuously feed on zooplankton. The dorsal surface of their silver bodies is streaked with deep yellow and the shoal provides a spectacle of silver and gold when their colours catch the sunlight at the surface.

Fusilierfish (*Paracaesio sp.*)
Fusiliers are most interesting to watch when they visit a cleaner-fish station. They flash their colours on and off and turn a darker colour as they are cleaned.

Electric-blue Damselfish (*Pomacentrus coeruleus*)

Damselfish belong to the family Pomacentridae and are closely related to clownfish. They include a wide variety of species, many of which are popular with aquarium enthusiasts.

The electric-blue damselfish reaches a maximum length of 9 cm and their usual territory is among the tips of staghorn coral. They seem to prefer sheltered areas and can sometimes be found excavating among the rubble on reef slopes. They are omnivorous feeders preying on zooplankton and small crustacea as well as feeding on algae.

Electric-blue Damselfish
(*Pomacentrus coeruleus*)
Identified by the vertical black stripe through its eye and the black oscellus at the base of the dorsal fin, the electric-blue damsel is also called the blue devil damselfish due to its pugnacious behaviour in aquaria.

Sergeant Major
(*Abudefduf sexfasciatus*)
Sometimes called the scissor-tailed sergeant major because of the shape of its tail, this species can also be identified by the six vertical stripes on its body. Sergeant majors feed in schools on plankton and seaweed. They are also opportunistic scavengers.

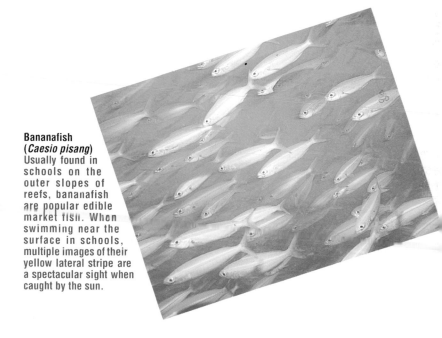

Bananafish
(*Caesio pisang*)
Usually found in schools on the outer slopes of reefs, bananafish are popular edible market fish. When swimming near the surface in schools, multiple images of their yellow lateral stripe are a spectacular sight when caught by the sun.

Striped Catfish (*Plotsus lineatus*)
In some species of catfish, juvenile forms may school whereas the adult forms do not. Catfish are bottom feeders. The sensitive whiskery barbels on their lower jaws are responsible for their common name.

115

Monastrea sp.
Inspected at close quarters, the surface of this massive reef building coral resembles a series of mini volcanoes. The polyps are not visible in this photograph, but when expanded for feeding they are so small that they appear as short, delicate tufts.

Apart from corals and algae, numerous invertebrate life forms inhabit the reef and each has its part to play in the complex pattern of inter-relationships that maintain the homeostasis of the coral reef ecosystem. Invertebrate organisms described in this section of the guide represent the major groups of marine invertebrates, ie: Porifera (sponges), Platyhelminths (flatworms), Annelids (segmented worms), Crustaceans (crabs, prawns, etc), Molluscs (shellfish and squid), Bryozoans (sea mats), Echinoderms (starfish, brittle stars, sea urchins, feather stars and sea cucumbers) and Tunicates (sea squirts).

More Than Meets the Eye
At first sight this small patch of reef looks like the habitat of beautiful orange sun corals and blue sponges. But in the gaps and crevices formed by their elaborate body forms, many tiny inconspicuous organisms such as flatworms, segmented worms, crustaceans, molluscs and echinoderms make their home.

MAJOR INVERTEBRATE GROUPS

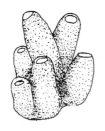

SPONGES

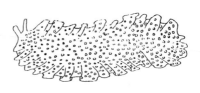

FLATWORMS

SEGMENTED WORMS

CRUSTACEANS

MOLLUSCS

ECHINODERMS

SPONGES (PORIFERA)

Members of the Phylum Porifera are better known by their common name: sponges. Sponges are the oldest and the most simple multicellular invertebrate organisms and they might be most aptly described as 'animal sieves'. They have neither internal organs nor body systems as such, only modified cells. Sponges are filter feeders. They draw in water through numerous tiny holes in their body walls and, after filtering out and ingesting the organic food content, the remaining water is expelled through one of the larger holes on the body surface.

In most reefs, sponges can be found in every conceivable variety of colours, shapes and sizes. They inhabit sheltered rock surfaces and reef crevices where there is less competition for light. Sponges can be described as simple or complex. Some growth forms they take are encrusting, branching, or columnar in appearance. For a long time, sponges were thought to be plants because they do not show obvious responses to stimuli.

Sponges are important in the ecosystem. Due to their sessile habit and porous structure they are veritable 'hotels' for other marine organisms. The labyrinth of tunnels that make up their bodies furnishes a perfect habitat for many small invertebrates such as brittlestars, crabs and worms.

The soft bodies of sponges acquire their shape and form from an elastic network called spongin or from small, jagged, glassy or carbonate structures called spicules, or from both. Because spicules are so sharp and unpleasant to eat, sponges are unpalatable to many surface grazers such as molluscs. Spicules are also sharp enough to pierce human flesh and they can be a source of great discomfort if they become embedded in the skin. It is wise, therefore, to handle sponges only when wearing protective gloves.

The colourful array of sponges pictured here are encrusting a dead coral head. Close examination reveals that such a sponge mass is a veritable 'hotel' for smaller organisms. Many types of sponges are also active coral borers, thus altering the profile of the substrate on which they grow.

THE STRUCTURE OF A GENERALISED SPONGE

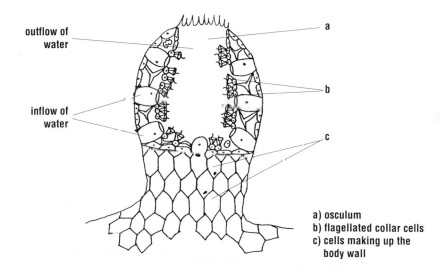

outflow of water

inflow of water

a) osculum
b) flagellated collar cells
c) cells making up the
   body wall

Organ-pipe Sponge
Sponges that grow in what looks like a cluster of hollow tubes are often called organ-pipe sponges. Tubes may reach 30 cm in height and are able to pump large quantities of water through their body mass. It is estimated that a single tube sponge of 10 cm in height can pump about 150 litres of water daily.

Organ-pipe Sponge
A closer look at an organ-pipe sponge reveals the uneven outer surface and the presence of numerous tiny holes (or pores) through which the sponge takes in water. The internal cavity of each tube is convoluted, thus enlarging the internal suface area. The large exhalant pore at the top of the tube is called the osculum.

Neptune's Cup Sponge

The Neptune's cup sponge or bucket sponge is a giant among the sponges. It can grow to a diameter of more than one metre. Commonly associated with this large sponge are small white sea cucumbers (synaptids) which are seen here clinging to its outer surface. As water is being drawn in through the small pores that penetrate the sponge's body wall, mucus and detritus food material that cannot pass through the pores collects on the outer surface. Hence, a convenient supply of food is available for the sea cucumbers.

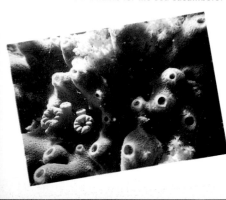

Blue Sponge

Yet another kaleidoscope of sponges mixed with *Tubastrea* and other corals. The small inhalant openings and the larger exhalant openings (oscula) are clearly visible in these specimens. Water that has already circulated through the sponge (and is therefore depleted of food particles and oxygen) is expelled through the oscula.

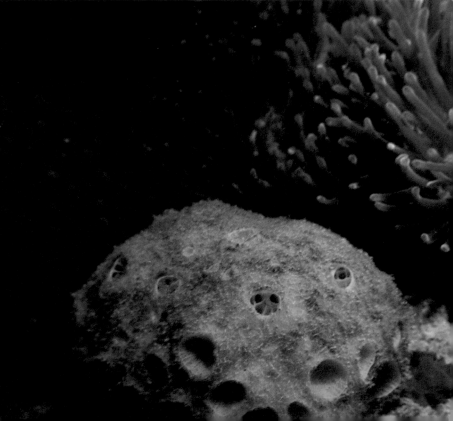

Encrusting Sponge

This sponge mass is not only encrusting the rock substrate on which it is living, but it is also growing mini-colonnades upward into the current. Some species of sponge take on different forms at different depths, locations and habitats. This makes identification difficult, even for experts.

Green Sponge

The supportive lattice-like skeletal structure of this green sponge is conspicuous in the living organism and will faithfully retain the form of the animal's body after its death. The tough skeletal structure of sponges renders them unpalatable to many invertebrate grazers.

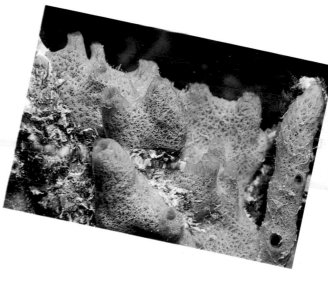

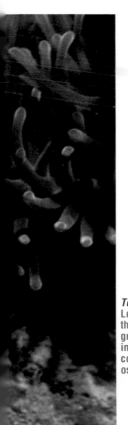

Tethya sp.

Looking like a small pitted orange which is in the process of distintegration, *Tethya* tends to grow among grass beds or in sandy patches in shallow water. *Tethya* is often seen almost completely covered in sand with only the oscular openings visible.

FLATWORMS (PLATYHELMINTHS)

Flatworms are fairly primitive in structure and most are aquatic. Marine flatworms found on local coral reefs belong to an order of flatworms referred to as Polyclads – meaning 'many (types of) clothing'. This term aptly depicts the appearance of the majority of tropical flatworms. They appear not only in a great variety of hues but also in a kaleidoscope of spots, stripes and mottled patterns. Few are pelagic and because their habitat is often in mud, under stones, or among crevices created by seaweed and sponges, even common specimens of flatworms may go unnoticed.

Flatworms are small and leaf like, sometimes with highly undulated edges to their body. Few species exceed 5 cm in length and they have no visible appendages except for small tentacles present on some species. The underside of the body is covered with minute hair-like structures called cilia. The cilia play an important role in movement over a solid surface. Assisted by mucous secretions and minute contractions of the body muscles, the cilia propel the organism in a smooth, gliding movement.

Polyclads can also swim, but they are unable to swim independently of the current. If they are swept off a rock or are disturbed in any way, the body muscles contract more forcefully in a sinuous, pulsating movement which causes the flatworm's body to move along in a wave-like motion.

Little is known about the habits of tropical marine flatworms and many are yet to be identified and named. They have been observed to feed on small invertebrates present on coral and sponge substrates. The mouth is on the ventral surface of the body and a tube or muscular pharynx protrudes to ingest their food which is partly digested outside the body.

Polyclads are hermaphroditic but they do not self-fertilise. A brief mating ritual is enacted and an elaborate set of copulatory organs ensures success in internal fertilisation by another individual of the same species. Eggs are laid in a protected location by both members of the copulating pair.

The genus *Pseudoceros* is well represented in the Indo-Pacific region. Members of this genus display a truly remarkable variety of exotic colours and patterns. Defenceless in other respects, the bright colours of flatworms serve as a deterrent to predators. This is because exotic colouration is associated with toxicity in many other invertebrate species.

Purple-spotted Flatworm
The characteristic bright colouring of tropical marine flatworms, such as this purple-spotted specimen, warns would-be predators that their mucous covering contains toxins.

Thysanozoon flavomaculatum
Bordered with white, this velvety black flatworm is dotted with slightly protruding bright yellow spots. This species is common in Malaysian waters and one of the easiest to identify.

Pseudoceros buskii
Predominantly black with a bright yellow border, this species is less colourful than other flatworms of the Indo-Pacific.

Pseudoceros bedfordi
Pseudoceros bedfordi is a spectacularly marked species that is frequently seen gliding over coral heads or occasionally swimming with graceful undulating movements.

Pseudoceros corallophilus
This is yet another species of the genus *Pseudoceros* that inhabits reefs in the Indo-Pacific. The undulating swimming movements typical of flatworms is clearly shown here. Some divers mistakenly refer to flatworms as Spanish dancers. However, this common name should be reserved for the nudibranch mollusc known as *Hexabranchus* which is much larger than any of the flatworms.

SEGMENTED WORMS (ANNELIDS)

Apart from flatworms, worms most often encountered on the reef are segmented worms or members of the phylum Annelida. Unlike the segmented worms that are free-living and burrow in the sand on the beach, most worms found on the coral reef are stationary in habit. Even so, despite their small and stationary habit, reef-dwelling annelids are among the most intriguing of the reef's attractions.

Christmas Tree Worm (*Spirobranchus giganteus*)

Christmas tree worms are filter feeders commonly found embedded in coral heads on the upper, sun-lit parts of coral heads. They build a calcareous tube embedded in the coral. From this secure position they protrude the familiar, colourful, feathery, spiral display.

The paired feathery structures or radioles are variously coloured and not only serve as external gills but also assist in feeding. Movement of the radioles creates a current which attracts food particles. After mixing the food particles with a mucous substance, it is then directed to the centrally positioned mouth. If disturbed, the Christmas tree worm will rapidly withdraw the external radioles and seal off the tube opening with a special flap called an operculum.

A SERPULID WORM

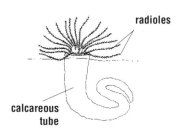

radioles

calcareous
tube

**Christmas Tree Worm
(S*pirobranchus giganteus*)**
Also called the bottle-brush tube worm, a close look at an individual Christmas tree worm reveals the paired feathery structures called radioles. The tongue-like flap visible to the lower left of the tube opening is called the operculum. This structure acts as a kind of lid, effectively sealing the entrance to the tube when the worm retreats. A colourful array of these Christmas tree worms adds a point of interest to the surface of the smooth Porites coral. The larval form of the Christmas tree worm bores into the coral and forms a calcareous tube in which the adult eventually lives.

126

Feather Duster Worm
(*Sabellastarte indica*)
The feather duster worm lives in a flexible membraneous or parchment-like tube from which it protrudes its feathery radioles. The giant nerve fibres present in these organisms are responsible for the rapid withdrawal motion when the animal is disturbed.

Feather Duster Tube Worm (*Sabellastarte indica*)

This common worm lives in a tube made of mud and mucus which is attached to corals. From the tube it protrudes a circular crown of feathery radioles which, in larger specimens, can reach a diameter of 8 cm. The radioles function much like those in the Christmas tree worm described above. In the feather duster worm, branches of the radioles are banded with a pale reddish-brown forming a delicate whorl-like display. A passing disturbance will guarantee that this fine display is withdrawn with amazing rapidity!

Feather Duster Worm
(*Sabellastarte indica*)
The radioles of the feather duster worm are frequently banded or speckled and when fully displayed can reach 8 cm across. The radioles serve a dual purpose. As well as having a respiratory function, they trap minute food particles and direct them to the central mouth.

Feather Duster Worm
(*Sabellastarte indica*)
Also called the fan worm, the feather duster tube worm lives a sedentary life. With its tube embedded below the surface of its coral enclave it depends on its fine display of radioles for feeding, respiratory and sensory functions.

White Sabellid (*Sabella sp.*)

The tube opening and the pair of fine feathery radioles are clearly visible in this white sabellid worm. Like most sabellids, this species builds a mud and mucous tube in sandy or muddy areas of the ocean bed.

Delicate Sabellid (*Sabella pavonina*)

The long mud and mucous tube of this sabellid worm is clearly visible. In this species the radioles protruding from the aperture of the tube are delicate in form and colour.

White Bristleworm

The segmented structure of this free-living annelid is clearly evident in this ragworm specimen. Each segment of its millipede-like body bears paired appendages or bristles. The head-end is equipped with complex mouth parts and antennae. Ragworms can typically be found in shallow muddy areas.

Spoonworm

Classified into a completely different group from the other worms illustrated here, spoonworms are unsegmented worms belonging to the Phylum Echiura. The anterior end, seen here protruding from the surface of the sand, is equipped with a ciliated, grooved proboscis which is used in feeding. Although the entire phylum consists of only about 130 species, Echiurians are ubiquitous bottom dwellers, being found at a range of depths burrowing in sand, rock and coral crevices.

CRUSTACEANS

Many of the larger crustaceans are better known for their gastronomic attraction than for their biological interest. Marine crustaceans are, however, handsome in their own right and they have interesting habits. Among the marine crustaceans found on the reef are numerous varieties of barnacles, prawns, crayfish and crabs.

Goose-necked Barnacle

For many years biologists classified barnacles as molluscs. It was not until the development of their larva was observed in detail that their close affinity to crustaceans was discovered. The larval form of barnacles look rather like tiny shrimp and are pelagic in habit. When they reach an optimal stage of development, they attach themselves to a chosen substrate by the back of their neck. They then develop further and begin to grow a series of overlapping calcareous plates. From then on the animal lives a sedentary life protruding its feathery feet to trap plankton forms for food.

Goose-necked Barnacle
When barnacles are covered with water and feeding, feathery jointed legs protrude from between the plates. These feathery structures strain food from the water. Because of their hard outer covering, barnacles are remarkably resistant to wave damage, temperature and chemical change as well as exposure to air.

Goose-necked Barnacle
Barnacles are composed of a soft body protected by a shell of upright plates called a carapace which close when the animal is exposed at low tide. The long fleshy neck (or peduncle) of goose-necked barnacles resembles the long neck of the bird after which it is named. All barnacles possess cement glands which secrete the necessary adhesive substance to attach them permanently to a particular location.

Goose-necked barnacles are well-known fouling organisms and are represented throughout the world. They are often seen on jetty pilings, the bottom of boats or attached to floating timber and other floating debris such as polystyrene and plastic. The type that grow in the South China Sea are particularly impressive in size.

Banded Coral Shrimp (*Stenopus hispidus*)

Also known as the barber shrimp, this tiny crustacean gets its name from the curious coincidence between the colouration of its body and the red and white poles that were the traditional guild marks of barbers' shops. A prominent feature of the animal is the third pair of appendages which are enlarged to form impressive red and white striped claws. The banded coral shrimp can grow to a length of approximately 5 cm and can be found living in pairs in small cracks in the reef.

Stenopus has the peculiar habit of feeding on small parasites that infest the scales of fish. This service is supplied to the mutual benefit of both parties.

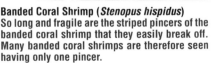

Banded Coral Shrimp (*Stenopus hispidus*)
So long and fragile are the striped pincers of the banded coral shrimp that they easily break off. Many banded coral shrimps are therefore seen having only one pincer.

The long white antennae are prominent signals to fish that might choose to take advantage of the cleaning services offered by the banded coral shrimp. The striped pincers are the reason that this shrimp is sometimes called the 'barber' shrimp.

Caridean Prawn

The rostrum or long extension of the carapace which protrudes forward at the top of the head of prawns is visible in this specimen, as are the large compound eyes.

Camel Shrimps

Shrimps differ from prawns in several ways. Shrimps have two pairs of pincers to the prawn's single pair. Shrimp also lack the forward projection of the shell between the eyes. Camel shrimps are an edible species of shrimp.

BASIC INTERNAL AND EXTERNAL FEATURES OF A GENERALISED CRUSTACEAN

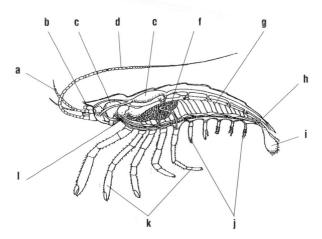

a) second antenna
b) eye stalk
c) stomach
d) first antenna
e) heart
f) digestive gland
g) muscle
h) telson
i) uropod
j) abdominal appendages
k) thoracic appendages
l) mouth

131

Slipper Lobster
(*Scyllarides squammosus*)
Unlike most species of lobster, the knobbly carapace of the nocturnal slipper lobster is flattened from top to bottom. Its body may reach 20 cm in length. The second pair of antennae is modified to form shield-shaped structures.

Painted Crawfish (*Panuliris sp.*)
Panulirus belongs to a group of crawfish known as spiny crawfish or lobsters. This group differs from the true Atlantic lobster in that its members lack powerful frontal pincers. *Panulirus* is one of the most handsome spiny lobsters and it is indigenous to Indo-Pacific reefs. It is seen here in its preferred location — under a ledge.

Spiny Crawfish
The heavily calcified, spiny exoskeleton provides the perfect armoured protection for the crawfish. Clearly visible here are the stalked compound eyes which are effective in locating food as well as sensing potential danger. Octopus are the major natural predators of crawfish.

Hermit Crabs

Hermit crabs are scavengers commonly seen along the shore-line. Although they have all the major characteristics of a crab, their coiled abdomen is softer and more vulnerable than that of most of their relatives. The diminished hind end of the hermit conveniently fits into the internal spiral of an empty snail shell.

The shell thereafter forms the hermit crab's protection and is carried everywhere the crabs goes. It is eventually exchanged for a larger one once the occupant outgrows it. When the hermit crab retreats into its shell, the front pincers carefully complete the protection by sealing off the shell's aperture. When the hermit crab needs to move around to feed, it protrudes its head and legs from the aperture and moves at an impressive pace.

Hermit Crab (*Dardanus sp.*)
Hermit crabs have large, soft abdomens and would be very vulnerable to attack were it not for the vacated mollusc shells which they use as their adopted home. They change shells from time to time as they outgrow each successive shell during their growing period.

Swimming Crabs (*Thalamita sp.*)

Crabs, like all of their crustacean relatives, have a hard external skeleton, jointed legs, complex mouth parts and stalked eyes. But, unlike their relatives the prawns and the lobsters, the body of most types of crabs is flattened dorso-ventrally (from top to bottom) rather than laterally (from side to side).

Swimming crabs are so called because of the structure of the last segment of the fifth pair of legs. This segment is oar shaped to aid in swimming. Swimming crabs can be mottled green or red and the fused body segments in their thorax (the carapace) can reach 10 cm across. Swimming crabs are omnivorous but defend themselves vigorously when attacked.

Sponge Crabs (*Dromia sp.*)

There are several species of sponge crabs belonging to the family Dromiidae. Members of this family have rather soft exoskeletons and large flat carapaces. Without an alternative means of protection they would easily fall prey to cuttlefish and octopus.

Dromia have a peculiar habit of covering their carapace with a single piece of living sponge which provides them with magnificent camouflage. The sponge seems unaffected by this peripatetic existence and continues growing quite normally. As the sponge grows, the crab becomes more and more enclosed by its growing 'overcoat'. Even though they never allow themselves to be separated from their sponge covering, sponge crabs do not attach the cover permanently to their carapace. In fact, they hold it in position with their last pair of appendages. When threatened, they will flatten themselves close to the substrate on which they happen to be standing so that little or nothing is visible except for the sponge.

If the crab is forcibly separated from its spongy cohabitant, it will cover itself hurriedly with anything in sight – animate or inanimate. Even a piece of paper or cardboard will suffice!

Sponge Crab (*Dromia sp.*)
Some species of crab, such as members of the genus *Dromia,* use other invertebrate organisms to camouflage their body. Curiously enough, the appropriated sponge continues to grow, even in its new peripatetic situation. Consequently, the crab is eventually almost entirely shrouded in its sponge 'overcoat'. Sponge crabs do not permanently fix their sponge camouflage to their body. Rather, the sponge is tirelessly held in place by a pair of the crab's posterior legs.

Swimming Crab (*Thalamita sp.*)
Swimming crabs can be identified by the flattened oar-shaped terminal segments of the fifth pair of legs.

134

Spider Crab (*Xenocarcinus sp.*)
Because they are so well camouflaged, spider crabs often go unnoticed. They are frequently found in pairs. The specimen shown here is secreted in the protective folds of a soft coral and it has assumed a strikingly similar colour.

Spider Crab (*Xenocarcinus sp.*)
There are many species of these so-called tiny 'spider crabs' present on the reef. Each is associated with another invertebrate organism which is usually sessile. *Xenocarcinus sp.* is seen here inhabiting a sea fan. It is scarcely visible due to its impressive camouflage.

135

Top Shell (*Trochus sp.*)
Several species of top shells inhabit shallow waters throughout the Indo-Pacific.
The shell of the larger species can reach a length of 15 cm. Some species have
a brilliantly hued nacreous layer which lines the shell. This pearl-like material
has traditionally been used for making buttons.

Chestnut Cowrie (*Cypraea spadicea*)
The jet-black mantle of the chestnut cowrie poses a striking contrast to the highly-lustred, chestnut-coloured shell. Cowries are unusual bivalves in that their mantle is bi-lobed. In their fully extended state, the two lobes virtually cover the shell.

MOLLUSCS (SOFT-BODIED ANIMALS)

Members of the phylum Mollusca that are of apparent importance on the reef can be categorized into three main groups: the gastropods (Class Gastropoda), the bivalves (Class Bivalvia) and the squid group (Class Cephalopoda).

Gastropods

Gastropods are the largest group of molluscs and most have a calcareous shell that protects the soft-bodied animal inside. Gastropods include univalves such as the abalone and the spiral-shelled snails as well as sea hares. Nudibranchs are also classified as gastropods but they are exceptional in that thay have no shell.

Gastropods move by means of a fleshy foot. As they move along, the grazing gastropods scrape away at the surface of rocks using a specialised structure called a radula. The radula is ridged or toothed and in some ways resembles the tongue of a cat. The radula can rasp or scrape away food literally as the gastropod moves along–hence the name 'gastro' (stomach) 'pod' (foot). In some gastropods the radula has modified into a dart or drill used for capturing prey.

Tiger Cowrie (*Cypraea tigris*)

The many species of cowrie are gastropods closely related to other spiral-shelled molluscs. They are most active at night when they can be seen browsing on algae on rock surfaces.

When cowries are moving, a fleshy part of the animal (called the mantle) is extended so that it envelopes the shell completely, thus camouflaging the animal whilst it feeds.

Specialised cells in the mantle continuously secrete a layer of protein that builds up a calcareous shell. This protein layer preserves the condition of the shell, protecting it from damage and giving it its glossy appearance.

Tiger Cowrie (*Cypraea tigris*)
Characterised by their black-spotted shell, tiger cowries are larger than most cowrie species. Mature adults can reach 15 cm in length. Juvenile cowries have thinner, cone-shaped shells. The shell gradually thickens and enlarges as the animal reaches maturity. As the cowrie moves, small projections called papillae are visible on the underside of the fleshy mantle. These papillae probably serve a sensory function as well as helping to camouflage the animal while it is feeding.

Arabian Cowrie (*Cypraea arabica*) – feeding
Cowries are omnivorous, feeding at night on corals, algae and sponges. On the underside of the mantle is the radula, a specialised feeding organ that enables the animal to graze on algae and sponges. The feeding mechanism of this Arabian cowrie is visible as it grazes on coral.

Murex (*Chicoreus sp.*)

Murex are spiral-shelled gastropods that are becoming increasingly rare because their spectacular shells are much sought after by shell collectors and souvenir vendors. If a Murex specimen is examined in its natural habitat, very little of the living animal will be visible except for a small portion of the fleshy foot protruding from the shell's operculum.

Certain features of the shell are, however, discernible. The portion of the shell between the apex (top) and the aperture (opening) is called the spire. Successive turns of the spire are called the whorl. The whorl of many species of Murex is adorned with spines, fronds and ridges. The beautiful colouration of the shell is not visible in the natural habitat as it is usually encrusted with algae and other organisms such as barnacles.

Murex feed by secreting acid from a gland in their foot and, with the help of the rasping radula, bore through the shells of other molluscs.

Murex (*Chicoreus sp.*)
Less common now than a decade ago, members of the family Muricidae can still be found in local waters. The shell's external surface is usually encrusted with sessile marine organisms which obscure its natural colours.

138

Venus Comb (*Murex sp.*)
Found occasionally in sandy regions, this beautiful species of Murex is notable for its prominent spines. The shell can be up to 10 cm in length. Like many other gastropods, the Venus Comb feeds mostly on bivalves. It attacks them by boring a hole through their shell with its radula.

Voluto (*Cymbiola nobilis*)
Among the largest and most avaricious of the gastropods found on the reef, volutes feed on bivalves. They subdue their prey by extending their fleshy foot and enclosing their victim which eventually weakens due to lack of oxygen. The bivalve is then forced to open the valves of its shell thus exposing its fleshy body which is promptly devoured by the volute.

139

Spider Conch (*Lambis lambis*)

Also called a scorpion conch, *Lambis lambis* has an unusual way of moving – resembling a 'pole vault'. When the extendible fleshy foot ventures out of the aperture, it will touch the sand and hook itself in. The heavy shell will be turned over before the conch continues its journey.

Spider Conch (*Lambis lambis*)

Two long eyestalks of the herbivorous spider conch are peeping out of the shell. They are patterned similarly to the shell and they appear to be keeping an 'eye' on where the 'foot' is heading.

Moon Snail (*Natica sp.*)

Called moon snails because of the shape and colour of their shell, these gastropods have smooth, thick, rounded shells. Their delicate white mantle is fully visible when the animal is moving. Moon snails prey on other gastropods. As they search for food, their route can be detected by the raised trail of sand created as they move just beneath the surface of the sea bed.

Chromodoris quadricolor
Nudibranchs are shell-less snails commonly referred to as 'sea-slugs'. Not many nudibranchs have common names but this striped member of the chromodorid group is appropriately called the 'pyjama nudibranch'. The radulas of nudibranchs assume a wide variety of forms according to the diet of the species.

Nudibranchs

Nudibranchs are clearly among the most decorative and fascinating marine molluscs. They belong to a subclass of the Gastropoda called Opisthobranchia or shell-less molluscs. Their name (which means 'naked gills') refers to the structure and location of their feathery gills which are exposed and carried dorsally on most species. Paired tentacles (rhinophores) can be found at the anterior end of many nudibranchs.

Nudibranchs are hermaphroditic meaning that all individuals function both as males and females. They reproduce when two fertile individuals pair off and connect on their right sides to receive sperm from each other, thus fertilising the eggs they will both eventually lay. The eggs are carefully laid in gelatinous loops or whorls that somewhat resemble flower petals.

There are about 2,500 species of nudibranchs worldwide and all of them inhabit intertidal regions or shallow subtidal waters. Most do not have a common name and because of their great diversity within the species, they are sometimes difficult even for experts to identify.

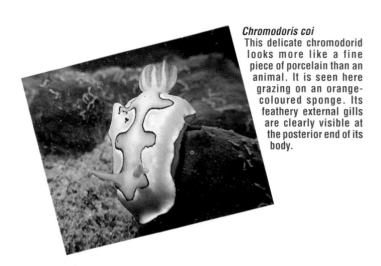

Chromodoris coi
This delicate chromodorid looks more like a fine piece of porcelain than an animal. It is seen here grazing on an orange-coloured sponge. Its feathery external gills are clearly visible at the posterior end of its body.

Jorunna sp.
Not all Doridaceans are brightly coloured. *Jorunna sp.* are a very delicate white, dotted with black speckled markings. The two small rosettes located on the blue sponge above the nudibranch are nudibranch eggs.

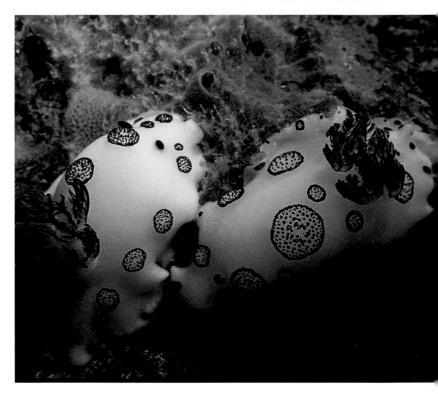

Nudibranchs mating
Nudibranchs are hermaphroditic, that is, each individual functions as both a male and female. As they mate, they line up head to tail and a tube connects the right sides of their body. Sperm is thus transferred to fertilise the eggs that both individuals will eventually lay.

Nudibranch Eggs
Nudibranch eggs are a common sight on the reef. The minute eggs are contained in egg capsules which are sealed in gelatinous ribbons arranged in loops or rosettes. They also appear in many different colours such as pink, red, white and even blue.

Aeolid Nudibranch
This long slender nudibranch is covered with blue or light purple processes. It is seen here on a sandy patch protruding its delicate orange-banded rhinophores.

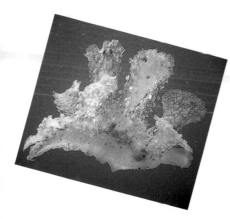

Melibe sp.
An atypical nudibranch in many respects, *Melibe sp.* is about 4–5 cm in length and so fragile it goes unnoticed to the less discerning eye. When not feeding, *Melibe* swims by repeatedly contorting its body in such a way that its head touches its tail. *Melibe* lack the usual radula to aid in feeding. Instead, the mouth is located at the bottom of a bell-shaped extension of the frontal veil. The bell-like sac acts as a suction cup, to imprison and suck in small organisms.

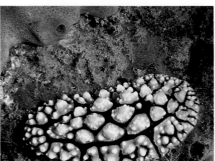

Phyllidia sp.
A common but less colourful nudibranch, *Phyllidia* has a tough, warty outer covering. Its gills are not immediately visible as they are located under the mantle. It is often seen actively feeding during the day.

Green-spotted Nudibranch (*Nembrotha kubaryana*)
Although it is not that common elsewhere in the region, this green-spotted black nudibranch is found in great numbers around Pulau Harimau (off Mersing, Malaysia).

Rainbow Nudibranch
This nudibranch has numerous protuberances (called cerata) on the surface of its body. These contain undigested nematocyst stinging cells from the hydroids on which it feeds. Its colourful body is a signal to potential predators that it is poisonous.

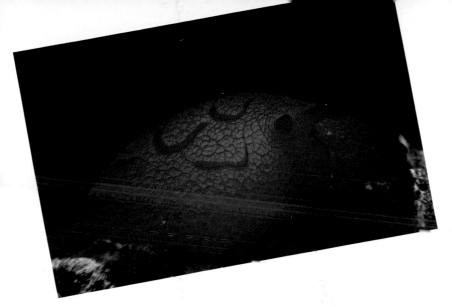

Pleurobranchus sp.
Pleurobranchus is a common Indo-Pacific species closely related to sea hares. It is notable for Its orangish-red colouration, its warty upper surface, and its fleshy mantle which is united with a veil of skin surrounding the mouth.

Sea Hare (*Aplysia sp.*)
Although they are very much larger in size, sea hares are shell-less molluscs closely related to nudibranchs. They exhIbit many similar features such as a fleshy body, paired, ear-like rhinophores, and a well-developed radula. The fleshy foot is often used to propel the animal in open water. *Aplysia* is easily identified by its greenish-brown, mottled colouration and the streaks of dark pigment of its body surface. Members of the genus are large, reaching 30 cm in length. They are often found in shallow waters among seaweed and seagrass beds.

Sea Hare (*Aplysia sp.*)
This close-up of the head of *Aplysia* reveals the characteristically paired rhinophores and a veil of tissue covering the mouth. Adult specimens of *Aplysia* are truly an awesome sight when in motion. They are active swimmers propelling themselves in open water by flapping specialised lobes bordering the foot.

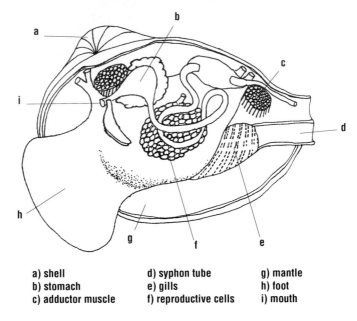

a) shell	d) syphon tube	g) mantle
b) stomach	e) gills	h) foot
c) adductor muscle	f) reproductive cells	i) mouth

Bivalves

Clams, scallops, oysters and mussels are bivalves since they have two parts to their shell which are held together by a type of hinge. Some bivalves are permanently sedentary while others are capable of moving from one location to another on the reef.

Giant Clam (*Tridacna sp.*)

The giant clam is a bivalve that is actually a form of cockle. In a striking parallel with the corals among which it lives, the giant clam has entered into a commensal relationship with certain species of algae.

In the giant clam, algae grow in special structures located in the fleshy mantle. In some respects these structures act like miniature greenhouses. By exposing the mantle and its algal gardens to bright sunlight in shallow, sunlit water, the giant clam is able to obtain almost all of its food and an ample supply of oxygen from its algal inhabitants, in spite of its primitive circulatory system. It is precisely because of the benefits of this association that the giant clam has been able to attain a size thousands of times larger than that of ordinary cockles.

Giant clams are filter feeders, but they also cultivate their own food manufacturing organisms (zooxanthellae) in the tissue of their fleshy mantle. When threatened, the two valves clamp together, sealing off and protecting the delicate mantle. Although this response quite effectively protects the vulnerable parts of their body from most predators, smaller specimens often fall prey to octopus.

Giant Clam (*Tridacna sp.*)
The most conspicuous feature of this giant bivalve is its bright blue mantle. The two valves of its massive fluted shell are almost entirely embedded in the surrounding coral.

Giant Clam (*Tridacna sp.*)
This shot of the mantle of *Tridacna* shows the exhalant syphon. The strikingly coloured mantle is a myriad of green which can be attributed, in part, to the presence of zooxanthellae in the mantle.

Fluted Oyster (*Pycnodonta hyotis*)

The fluted oyster is a bivalve that lives a rather sedentary life in the subtidal region of Indo-Pacific reefs. It can be identified by the zig-zag or fluted edges of the two valves of its shell.

Like the giant clam, the fluted oyster remains cemented to a hard substrate for the major portion of its life. The two shells are held together by a hinge and fit closely together around the soft body or mantle. The lower shell valve is cemented to the coral reef and often the entire shell is encrusted with corals and sponges. When opened, the two shells reveal a magnificently patterned mantle.

The fluted oyster is a filter feeder which derives its food from the plankton in seawater. Like all bivalves it has a unique filter system that involves two syphons. Water containing oxygen and microscopic organisms is drawn in through one of the tubes and directed to the gills. As the water is drawn through the gills, oxygen is removed and food particles stick to the surface of the gills. Tiny hairs on the gills then sweep these food particles into the mouth and stomach.

Fluted Oyster (*Pycnodonta hyotis*)

The 'V'-shaped edges of the fluted oyster's shell are probably responsible for its other common name, the zig-zag oyster. The two valves form a perfect fit when the organism tightly closes its shell. The uneven outer surface of the shell provides an ideal substrate for growth of sponges and other encrusting organisms.

Thorny Oyster (*Spondylus sp.*)

Sedentary in nature, this thorny oyster is barely visible with all the camouflage provided by the algae and sponges that are encrusting its shell. The first clue in detecting a thorny oyster embedded in a rock is often the colourful mantle. This is normally exposed to the current, to maximise possibilities for intake of food.

Fan-shell Scallop (*Atrina sp.*)

The shell of this fan-shell scallop is triangular and can reach 30 cm across. It is normally embedded in corals with only the attractively striped mantle visible when the animal feeds.

Horse Mussel (*Modiolus sp.*)

Like all mussels, the horse mussel has a thin shell attached to its substrate with threads arising from the foot. Its shell is long (45 cm) with an expanded convex posterior end resembling a horseshoe. The colourful mantle is seen here protruding from the partially opened valves.

148

Cephalopods

Cephalopods are a specialised group of predatory molluscs with soft bodies which, in many groups, are not protected by shells. They might be referred to as 'headfooted' molluscs because, strictly speaking, their foot is wrapped around their head. Other notable features of cephalopods include their well-developed nervous system, their rapid, hydraulically controlled 'reverse gear' movement and certain defence mechanisms which include release of an ink-like substance which blocks the vision of would-be predators.

Cuttlefish (*Sepia sp.*)

The short body of the cuttlefish is bordered with a lateral flap of tissue fringing the body. The head has ten tentacles, two of which are longer and more mobile than the rest. The two longer tentacles possess suckers which are specialised for capturing prey. The calcareous internal skeleton of cuttlefish (the cuttlebone) acts as a buoyancy aid.

Cuttlefish are noted for their sociable behaviour. They are also capable of perfecting their camouflage by instantaneously changing their colour to match their surroundings.

During the egg laying season, cuttlefish are often seen near the shore in pairs. After the eggs are fertilised the female carefully stores them in a protected place. Looking like bunches of white grapes, cuttlefish eggs are often seen suspended beneath coral slabs.

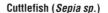

Cuttlefish (*Sepia sp.*)
Cuttlefish are sociable creatures and they will act playfully with gentle encouragement. Undulations of the lateral fin fringing the body allows for slow, deliberate, precise movement. In contrast, sudden jet-propelled movement is employed when cuttlefish capture prey or avoid predators.

Cuttlefish (*Sepia sp.*)
With tentacles curved downwards and eyes slightly closed, this cuttlefish appears to be on the defensive. An interesting feature of cuttlefish is the eye, which is fairly advanced compared to most invertebrates. Like most cephalopods, the nervous system of cuttlefish is also quite advanced.

EXTERNAL FEATURES OF CUTTLEFISH AND SQUID

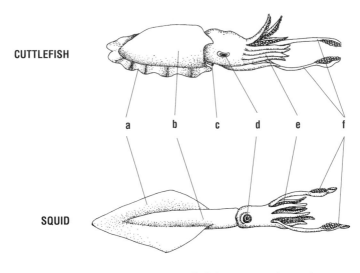

CUTTLEFISH

SQUID

a b c d e f

a) lateral fins   c) syphon   e) tentacles
b) body   d) eye   f) retractible tentacles
                                       with suckers

Cuttlefish (*Sepia sp.*)
Caught in the act of laying its eggs, this cuttlefish is depositing them in a characteristic location among the branches of coral. Referred to as sea grapes, cuttlefish eggs are white, spherical, and coated with a gelatinous substance.

Cuttlefish (*Sepia sp.*)
In an alert and attentive pose, this cuttlefish is obviously showing a great deal of interest in the photographer. Small, star-shaped pigmented cells in the skin of many cephalopods facilitate camouflage.

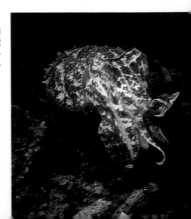

Squid (*Loligo sp.*)
This young squid is demonstrating the potential of its two oral tentacles which operate in a rapid scissor-like movement. Like the cuttlefish, the skin of squid is abundantly supplied with star-shaped chromatopores which allow a range of colour variation.

Squid (*Loligo sp.*)

Squid resemble cuttlefish in their basic body structure, except that they lack the undulating fringe encircling the body. Squid vary in size from a few centimetres to more than 40 metres in length.

From the anterior end of the animal protrude tentacles, one pair of which is greatly elongated. All the tentacles bear suckers which are modified to hold and catch prey. Once the prey is captured it is pulled into a beak-like mouth between the tentacles, torn apart by powerful jaws, then ingested.

The structure of the eye of the squid bears close resemblance to the human eye. The eyes even possess an upper eyelid!

Squid (*Loligo sp.*)
Squid are continuously active. This squid is pictured at night in reverse gear, jet-propelled motion. The squid's eyes assume an impressive brilliance when reflecting the light of a flashlight.

Octopus (*Octopus sp.*)

This nocturnal cephalopod is completely devoid of skeletal tissue. However, it has acquired other means of protection. For one thing, it can move rapidly and squeeze into tiny crevices of the reef, either to avoid predators or to pursue potential prey such as crabs or other crustaceans. Once an octopus has cornered its prey, it will entangle the animal with its arms and bite and kill the unfortunate creature with its jaws. Octopuses are also noted for their remarkable ability to change colour. This confuses predators and enables an octopus to conceal its whereabouts.

Octopus (*Octopus sp.*)
Unlike cuttlefish and squid which have a reduced internal shell, octopuses are shell-less molluscs. They have a short rounded body and eight tentacles which are equipped with a double row of suckers. Octopuses are able to squeeze into the tiniest crevice and are not often seen during the day. They have a well-developed sensory and nervous system and are nocturnal predators. They feed mainly on crabs and other crustaceans.

SEA MATS (BRYOZOA)

The name 'Bryozoa' is derived from two Greek words which together mean 'moss animals'. Because some species resemble an underwater carpet of moss, Bryozoans are also commonly called sea mats. They are colonial organisms which readily attach themselves to rocks, ship hulls, pier pilings, mollusc shells and the like. For this reason, they are regarded as fouling organisms.

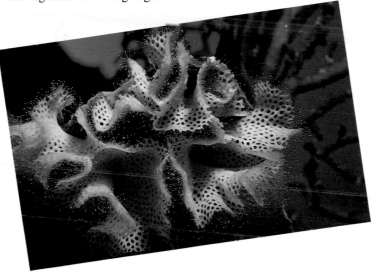

Bryozoans can be found in a great variety of forms. They can be leaf-like or bushy, but more often they take on an encrusting growth form. They are found from intertidal regions to great depths and are often the first organisms to colonise a sunken wreck or a newly exposed area. Bryozoan colonies of some Indo-Pacific species can measure up to 50 cm in diameter.

Individual organisms within the Bryozoan colony are minute animals called zooids. Each individual zooid sits in a small cell or honey comb-like cavity which can be horny, gelatinous or calcareous. Often the cavity is enclosed and protected by a cap. The tiny zooids are connected throughout the colony by a labyrinth of canals.

Bryozoans are extremely difficult to identify as they take on different forms depending on the surrounding environment and the depth at which they grow. In some cases, an electron microscope is required for exact identification.

Bryozoans live on plankton and organic particles present in the water. When feeding, the animal stretches forth a ring of ciliated tentacles which filter minute particles out of the water, eventually passing them down into the gut.

Bryozoans are hermaphroditic and the larva of some species are free swimming. This no doubt contributes to the ubiquitous nature of their varied habitat.

Black-banded Brittlestar
(*Ophideris superba*)
The black-banded brittlestar is a heavy-weight as far as brittlestars go. Its disc averages 2 cm whereas the tip-to-tip diameter can be 30 cm. *Ophideris superba* is one of the most common species of brittlestars in Singapore and Malaysian waters.

SPINY-SKINNED ANIMALS (ECHINODERMS)

Members of the Phylum Echinodermata include Asteroidea (starfish), Ophiuroidea (brittlestars), Echinoidea (sea urchins), Crinoidea (featherstars) and the Holothurioidea (sea cucumbers). Although diverse in form, many echinoderms have certain features in common, namely: a body structure that has five major discernible parts, a mouth located on the underside, a water vascular system, and tube feet. With the exception of sea cucumbers, echinoderms are radially symmetrical.

Present on the upper surface of all starfish arms are minute pincer-like structures called pedicellaria. These structures ensure that the surface of the arms stay free from algae or other would-be sources of infestation.

INTERNAL AND EXTERNAL FEATURES OF A STARFISH

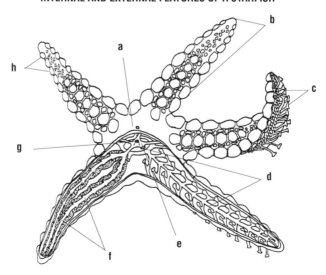

a) madreporite   d) water vascular system   g) anus
b) arm   e) stomach   h) scales
c) suckers   f) digestive system

Starfish (*Asteroidea*)

Crown-of-Thorns Starfish (Acanthaster planci)

The Crown-of-Thorns starfish is probably the largest, the most spectacular and the most venomous of all starfish found in the South China Sea. It can reach 50 cm in diameter and is distinguishable by its large size and the appearance of its numerous spiny arms or rays (up to 21 cm) which extend outwards from the bulky central disc that resembles a crown.

The variety of *Acanthaster* most commonly found on the reefs of the South China Sea has a greyish-blue and rust-coloured upper surface and a bright yellow undersurface. Both the upper and the under surfaces of the starfish are covered by thorn-like spines which are highly venomous.

The Crown-of-Thorns starfish feeds exclusively on hard corals. Like other starfish, its feeding mechanism is such that it is able to extrude its entire stomach through its mouth. The extruded stomach envelops the portion of coral it is about to consume and it secretes the necessary digestive juices to liquefy the coral tissue. The digested food mass, together with the stomach, is then sucked back in again. This method of external digestion is common to many starfish as they have no hard mouth parts to help them capture and ingest their prey.

Crown-of-Thorns Starfish (*Acanthaster planci*)
Here the crown-like body of *Acanthaster* is clearly evident. A mature Crown-of-Thorns can reach a diameter of 50 cm and have up to 23 arms or rays extending from its bulky disc. Both the upper and lower surfaces bear formidable thorn-like spines which vary from purplish to reddish brown colour.

Crown-of-Thorns Starfish
(*Acanthaster plancii*)
This close-up shot of the upper surface of *Acanthaster* clearly shows
the thorny spines after which the
species is named. The spines are
formidable in appearance as well as
size. Individual spines can reach 6
cm in length.

This close-up shot of its underside
shows the tube feet with yellow suck-
ered tips. The water vascular system of
starfish supplies water to the tube feet
via a series of canals. As it presses
against a moving object, water is withdrawn from the tube feet, resulting in a
suction effect. When water returns to
the canals, suction is released.

The recent increase in the numbers of *Acanthaster* observed by
divers in the South China Sea is a matter of some concern to con-
servationists. Crown-of-Thorns are well-known for the devastation
they cause to reefs. Although normally a nocturnal feeder, when the
population is large in a particular area, they also feed by day. In a
period of 24 hours, a single Crown-of-Thorns starfish can devour
large stretches of the reef, leaving behind white patches of dead coral
in its tracks. It has been estimated that an active Crown-of-Thorns
can devour as much as 50 sq cm of coral polyps every 24 hours.

Because of its devastating impact, *Acanthaster* is the subject of a
number of research projects being undertaken worldwide, most
notably in Australia. It is of obvious interest to marine biologists
to find out causes of recurrent increases in *Acanthaster* populations
and how their impact on the reef can be controlled.

Crown-of-Thorns is the only venomous asteroid. Researchers in
Australia have found that the toxin extracted from their spines may
have medicinal value. Under laboratory conditions, the extract
arrests the growth of tumours in some animals.

Peppermint Sea Star (*Fromia monilis*)
The peppermint sea star is a fairly common species. It has the
classical appearance of a starfish in that five arms can be seen radiating from a central disc. The red and white markings visible on
the arms are plates bearing spiny projections.

Peppermint Sea Star (*Fromia monilis*)
Small but attractive, this starfish's maximum
width is 8 cm. Large and small scale-like
coverings alternate along its arm edges.

Although they appear rigid on first impression, the arms of the peppermint sea star, in common with those of other starfish, are quite flexible and can act like pincers to aid in capturing small prey such as molluscs. By means of a suction effect made possible by the hydraulic system acting through the tube feet, the powerful muscular arms of *Fromia* are able to pry open bivalves and expose the soft body parts which offer a choice source of food.

Present on the upper surface of all starfish arms are minute pincer-like structures called *pedicellaria*. These structures ensure that the surface of the arms stay free from algae or other potential sources of infestation.

Blue Linckia (*Linckia laevigata*)

Blue Linckia's size has been recorded at around 40 cm in diameter. Noted for its habit of frequenting sunlit parts of the reef, *Linckia* is often found lying in shallow, flat, sandy areas or in coral rubble. The same species can also be found in an orangey-red colour.

Blue Linckia (*Linckia laevigata*)
Blue Linckia is a large brilliantly coloured starfish most commonly seen in sunny, shallow, sandy areas of the reef.

Linckia multiflora
A common starfish, *Linckia multiflora* reproduces by breaking off an arm which then regenerates into a new starfish. Little is known about what actually stimulates this process. In the first stage, the arm enlarges (as shown in this photograph) and literally walks away from the parent organism, severing itself at the base of the ray.

The newly-severed arm grows into four tiny buds or protusions which gradually grow to form the four additional rays needed to form a new organism. The severed ray of the 'parent' starfish regenerates to form the fifth ray and the parent animal is 'complete' again.

Cushion Star (*Culcita nouvaeguineae*)
Despite their puffy appearance, cushion stars are flexible in their movements. They are able to squeeze water out of their rays and thus reduce their bulkiness. They can even contort their disc sufficiently to turn themselves the right way up if they are turned upside down by the wave action.

Cushion Star (*Culcita nouvaeguineae*)

Sometimes called the pincushion star, the structure of *Culcita nouvaeguineae* is unlike any other genus in its group. It is comparatively bulky, pentagonal in shape, and puffy in appearance. Its structure on first sight seems to be highly unusual for a starfish – that is, it appears to be composed of all disc and no arms.

The upper surface of *Culcita* has a velvety appearance patterned with large contrasting blotches. Adult specimens can reach a size of 40 cm in diameter. Although not much is known about their feeding habits, they are thought to be slow coral feeders.

Cushion Star
(*Culcita nouvaeguineae*)
The underside of the cushion star reveals a five-part structure which identifies the organism as an echinoderm. Protruding from the five grooves on the underside of the cushion star are tube feet. These delicate structures are protected by scales lining the ridges.

Cushion Star (*Culcita nouvaeguineae*)
The pentagonal appearance of the cushion star gives only the slightest indication that the organism is related to other starfish. Variation in colour and markings typical of the species can clearly be seen by comparing the two specimens pictured here.

Nodular Starfish (*Nidorella armata*)

The nodular starfish has five short, blunt rays which turn up slightly at the tips. The term 'nodular' refers to the large conical spines on the dorsal surface. These spines are more conspicuous in younger specimens where they radiate uniformly from the centre of the disc along the upper ridge of each ray. In mature specimens, the nodes are worn down and additional ones appear between the five original rows.

The most common colour of the nodular starfish is grey with darker protrusions. Adult specimens may reach 20 cm across. Their outer skeletal structure is firm, their disc and arms quite bulky.

Nodular Starfish (*Nidorella armata*)
The nodular starfish, often found in shallow waters on sandy, flat areas, is flexible enough to move and feed, but is more rigid than other starfish.

Common Starfish *(Protoreaster nodosus)* feeding on a sea urchin
The mouth opening of starfish is centrally located on the underside of the body. Regardless of the size of the starfish, the mouth is small and possesses no hard mouth parts to assist in capturing its prey.

Brittlestars (*Ophiuroidea*)

Brittlestars are close relatives of starfish as they belong to the same class of echinoderms: Stelleroidea. Compared to starfish, brittlestars have a much smaller central disc which is distinct from the long tapering arms.

The tube feet of brittlestars are used for feeding and not for movement, as is the case with starfish. Instead, the highly mobile arms are used to facilitate movement over corals and other surfaces. The mouth is located on the underside of the disc and there is no anus. Waste is eliminated through the mouth.

Green-banded Brittlestar (*Ophiarachnella gorgonia*)
The green-banded brittlestar can be found on rocky shores and on coral reefs. Each of its arms has 8-13 spines. Broad green bands decorate its arms. Its disc also has green or tan markings.

As the name suggests, the arms of brittlestars are rather brittle and liable to break when the animal is handled. If this happens, the broken arm will continue actively wriggling (apparently acting as a decoy) while the rest of the brittlestar crawls hastily away. This escape mechanism, together with its remarkable property of regeneration, may well be an aspect of the evolutionary development of brittlestars that has contributed to their success. An entire new organism can regenerate from one arm, if the broken arm happens to be attached to a sizeable portion of the disc.

Some brittlestars inhabit the cavities and canals of large sponges. At night, their long arms can be seen extended from the opercula as they search for food. Like most brittlestars, the green-banded brittlestar is a nocturnal omnivore. During the day it is likely to be found tucked away under a rock or wedged in a coral crevice.

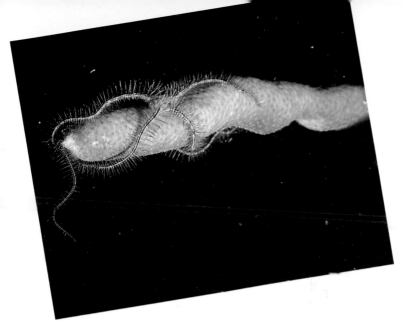

Hairy Brittlestar
This brittlestar is entwined around a coral protrusion. The fine, hair-like spines fringing the arms are characteristic of many species of brittlestar.

Basketstar (*Astroboa sp.*)

Having the same basic structure as their relatives the starfish and the brittlestars, the five main branches or arms of the basketstar are often obscured because of the way in which they are subdivided into a multitude of finer branches which terminate in tendril-like tips.

Basketstars feed nocturnally. They emerge at night to unfold mesh-like arms as they attempt to catch small swimming prey. The tips of the branches are extremely fragile and because of their delicate structure they are sometimes confused with stinging hydroids.

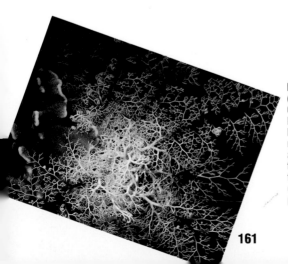

Basketstar (*Astroboa sp.*)
Common to the Indo-Pacific, this territorial basketstar is a nocturnal feeder. It emerges and spreads out its tendril-like arms to form a mesh which is effective in capturing prey.

161

Sea Urchins (*Echinoidea*)

Sea urchins are members of the Subphylum Echinozoa which also includes sea cucumbers. Their affinity with other groups of echinoderms is apparent from their radial symmetry as well as from the fact that they possess tube feet and pedicellaria. The specialised features of sea urchins include an external skeleton (called a test) as well as a centrally located mouth on the underside and an anus on the upper surface. Depending on the species, movable spines of various sizes are attached to the test. Pincer-like pedicellaria are present between the spines. Tube feet, much like those on the undersurface of starfish, protrude through the test.

Urchins are primarily grazers. They feed on the fine layer of filamentous algae growing on the surface of dead corals. Associated with the mouth of sea urchins is a specialised feeding mechanism known as the Aristotle's lantern. This specialised feeding mechanism is peculiar to sea urchins. It consists of a complex arrangement of muscles and plates surrounding the circular mouth. The overlapping plates are effective in scraping off and masticating the urchin's food so that it can be easily ingested.

Black Long-spined Sea Urchin
(*Diadema setosum*)
Apart from their long spines, the most striking feature of *Diadema setosum* is the luminescent purple blob that is located in the centre of the upper side of the test. This is the anal sac and its purple colour is made even more conspicuous by a prominent orange spot in its centre.

Black Long-spined Sea Urchin (*Diadema setosum*)

The long-spined sea urchin is abundant along the sandy seaward edges of reef flats and groups of them are often massed together in large colonies. The long slender black spines measure up to 20 cm in length and are very brittle, breaking off at the slightest contact. The tips of the spines are barbed and sharp enough to penetrate a diver's wet suit. Once they are lodged in the skin, the tips of the spines are almost impossible to remove. They then become a source

of pain and discomfort for the unfortunate victim.

Like most sea urchins, the mouth of *Diadema* is centrally located on the undersurface and the anus on the upper surface. The anus of *Diadema* is marked with a bright purple, almost luminescent sac which is sometimes mistaken for an eye.

Diadema sp. (*albino*)
Because of its white spines, this albino variety of the long-spined sea urchin is sometimes mistaken for a different species.

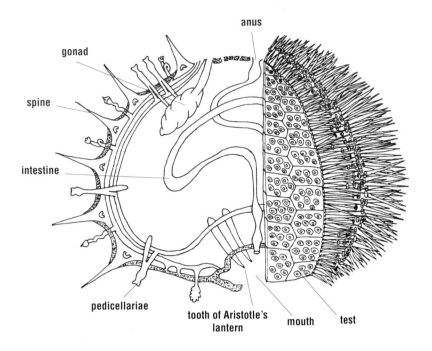

Sea Urchin (*Echinothrix sp.*)

Echinothrix is similar in appearance to *Diadema* except that there are two distinct sets of spines. The longer spines are quite robust and banded with shades of rust, light brown or green. The shorter spines are slender, pale coloured and regarded as poisonous.

Sea urchin spines will work in unison to protect the sea urchin from danger. They are capable of a wide range of rotation as they are attached to the test by a type of structure similar to the ball and socket joint in the human skeleton.

Echinothrix sp. (close-up of anal sac)
Granules and plates are visible on the surface of the distended membraneous anal sac of *Echinothrix*. Fecal material is stored in the sac before it is released into the surrounding environment.

Banded Long-spined Sea Urchin (*Echinothrix*)
Two sets of spines are present on *Echinothrix*: the banded (primary) and the darker, but shorter (secondary) spines. Even though they are not evident in this picture, all sea urchins have five double rows of tube feet which protrude through holes in the test. These tube feet are used for locomotion.

Short-spined Red Sea Urchin
This beautiful but uncommon species of sea urchin is found in deeper parts of the reef slope. The black spines are believed to be poisonous.

Flower Urchin (*Toxopneustes pileolus*)
Beautiful to look at but lethal to touch, the flower urchin can cause intense pain if handled. Compared to other urchins, the flower urchin's spines are small and inconspicuous among the fleshy pedicellaria that resemble flower petals. A species that is indigenous to the Indo-Pacific, it can reach a maximum diameter of 15 cm.

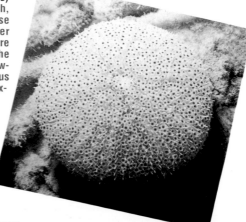

Alabaster Sea Cucumber (*Opheodesoma sp.*)
Opheodesoma is a synaptid or soft-bodied, worm-like sea cucumber. It is relatively small compared to other sea cucumbers in the region, reaching a maximum length of 20 cm. Seen here in a cluster clinging to the outer surface of a Neptune's cup sponge, it conveniently obtains a ready supply of food. At the same time, it is helpful to the sponge by keeping open the tiny pores through which the sponge ingests plankton-laden sea water.

Sea Cucumbers (*Holothurioidea*)

Sea cucumbers exist in enormous numbers littering the sea bed from the seashore to great depths. As their name suggests, these organisms are cucumber-shaped but this is where the similarity ends. Sea cucumbers have elongated, muscular, flexible bodies with a mouth at one end and an anus at the other. They move by means of tube feet which extend in rows from the underside of the body. The tentacles surrounding the mouth are actually tube feet that have been modified for feeding. Feeding takes place as the tube feet shovel sand and mud containing dead organic matter into the mouth.

Most sea cucumbers have a remarkable capacity for regenerating their body parts. When attacked, they shed sticky, thread-like structures which are actually parts of their gut. These structures then quickly regenerate so that the animal can continue as normal. The body wall of some sea cucumbers contains a toxin called holothurin. The unpleasant taste of holothurin probably accounts for the fact that sea cucumbers have relatively few natural predators.

STRUCTURE OF A SEA CUCUMBER

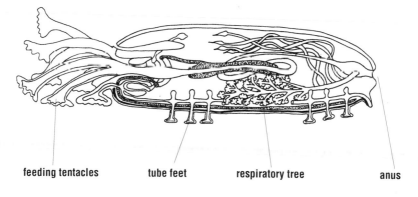

feeding tentacles   tube feet   respiratory tree   anus

Black and White Sea Cucumber (*Bohadschia graeffei*)
One of the most attractive sea cucumbers, *Bohadschia graeffei* reaches a length of 60 cm. Here the black, leaf-shaped feeding tentacles are searching for food on the surface of the coral and sponge substrate.

167

Black and White Sea Cucumber
(*Bohadschia graeffei*)
A close-up look at the anterior region of the underside of the leaf-shaped feeding tentacles.

Marbled Sea Cucumber
A smooth-skinned sea cucumber with an attractive marbled appearance. Its sticky surface causes sand to adhere easily.

Leopardfish Sea Cucumber
(*Bohadschia argus*)
Notable for its conspicuous markings, *Bohadschia argus* is often seen on coral sands in the region. It is seen here in a defence posture having eviscerated thick white sticky threads called Cuvierian tubules. These threads will regenerate within a few days.

Edible Sea Cucumber
(*Halodeima edulis*)
Black on top and pink below, the edible sea cucumber is less common now than it was five years ago. It is sometimes seen close to the shoreline with patches of sand adhering to its surface.

Prickly Redfish Sea Cucumber (*Thelenota ananas*)

THis sea cucumber is fairly common to the Indo-Pacific region and is seen on sand flats near local reefs. It is a relatively large species (sometimes exceeding one metre). Its name is obviously attributed to the large multilobed thorn-like structures (or papillae) projecting from its skin. The many crevices among these thorns create an ideal environment for small commensal organisms.

Grey Leathery Sea Cucumber (Holothuria sp.)

This relatively unattractive species is also rather inactive. Its tough skin contains spicules which render it unpalatable both to natural predators and to collectors of local delicacy called 'trepang' or 'beche de mere'.

Mottled Sea Cucumber

This worm-like sea cucumber is a soft-bodied synaptid which is mottled in appearance. It reaches a length of two metres and is well known for its apparently sticky surface. Actually the stickiness is due to spicules in the body wall which causes it to adhere to anything with which it comes into contact.

Sea Apple

The modified tube feet associated with the mouth of the sea apple resemble tendril-like branches. The animal is seen perching on rock ledges trapping floating organic materials with its tendrils outstretched.

Feather Stars (*Crinoidea*)

Feather stars are echinoderms that are immediately recognisable by their long feather 'arms' which extend outwards in a star formation from a central structure known as a cup.

Most species of feather stars are highly mobile, clinging on to their substrate by means of specialised tubular, hair-like structures called cirri. The arms of feather stars are plume-like. Fringing the jointed arms are smaller, brightly coloured structures called pinnules. If these pinnules are inspected very closely, they are seen to be alternately arranged on opposite sides of the central stalk rather like the pinnules of a bird's feather.

Feather stars feed at night by crawling to a vantage point in the current. Their feathery arms sway in the current and organic particles and plankton stick to the pinnules and flow down mucous canals into their centrally located mouth.

During the day, feather stars can be found under a ledge with their arms coiled inwards. In this resting position, tiny fish or other creatures can be found tucked snugly inside the feathery arms.

Red Feather Star (*Himerometra sp.*)
Himerometra move by means of jointed cirri. The arms stretch upward and tucked inwards to reduce possibilities of damage as the organism relocates.

Feather Star (*Himerometra*)
This crinoid is clinging onto the coral by means of its jointed lower appendages known as cirri. Five main arms extend upwards from the central cup, branching repeatedly. Some types of feather stars have 30 or more arms, each about 10cm long. The arms of *Himerometra sp.* are more robust than those of other species of feather stars.

170

Red Feather Star
(*Himerometra sp.*)
This top view of *Himerometra sp.* shows the feather star in resting position. The folded arms provide a convenient hiding place for small fish or invertebrates.

Ten-armed Feather Star (*Colometra sp.*)
Colometra sp. normally has 10-20 arms with short, robust pinnules. They can be white or varying shades of gold or brown. These two specimens are in characteristic feeding pose with short arms outstretched.

Banded Feather Star
(*Lampometra sp.*)
The banded feather star is a night-active species exclusive to the Indo-Pacific. The diameter of its arms can reach 15 cm. In some species the cirri bear small projections. The blunt, tufted lips of the arms are characteristic of this species.

171

Botrylloides sp.
This Indo-Pacific species is a fleshy, encrusting colonial tunicate. It can be identified by rows of individual organisms surrounding common ovoid exhalant
openings in a horseshoe or incomplete circular pattern.

SEA SQUIRTS (TUNICATES)

Because of their sac-like body, sea squirts or tunicates are often mistaken for sponges. Actually, they are much more advanced forms of life. Tunicates belong to a subphylum of the Chordata called Urochordata, meaning that they possess chordate characteristics in the larval stages of their life cycle.

Tunicates begin their life as free-living tadpole-like organisms but, in time, most attach themselves to a rock or coral head, lose their 'tail', and settle down to assume the form of tiny stationary sac-like structures. On first appearances, sea squirts look simple in structure but, on closer inspection, two openings or syphons can be identified. One of the openings is fringed by tiny tentacles which draw water and food particles into the sac-like body. Waste materials leave from the other (exhalant) outlet. Tunicates also possess a gut, a heart and a circulatory system. If disturbed, a sea squirt will shrink drastically, forcing water out through both the syphons.

Most tunicates are hermaphroditic. Fertilisation takes place either inside the exhalent siphon or in open water.

Yellow Sea Squirt (*Polycarpa sp.*)
The yellow sea squirt is a solitary tunicate that can reach a maximum size of 15 cm. *Polycarpa* is characterised by its thick, tough, occasionally brightly coloured outer covering which often bears irregular swellings. The exhalant syphon is clearly visible half way down the body of the organism.

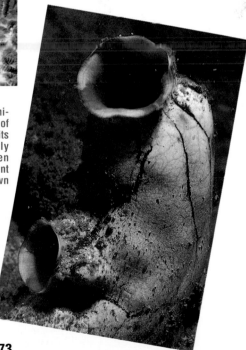

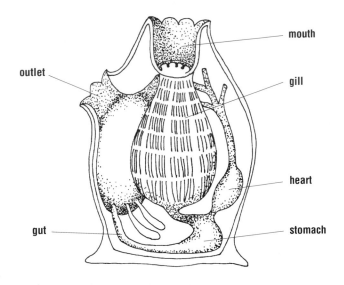

Green Grape Ascidian (*Didemnum sp.*)

This green colonial tunicate is often mistaken for a sponge. Sometimes individual members of the colony are spherical in shape, resembling the grapes after which they are named. In other specimens they are elongated. The external appearance is that of a white/green marble. Appearing at intervals in the colonies are small openings which reveal the vivid green of the interior of the animal.

Further inspection of these green apertures reveal fine membraneous threads which form the interior chambers of the organism.

LARVAL STAGE OF SEA SQUIRT

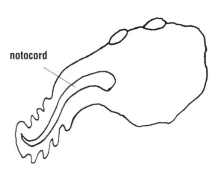

Ascidian (*Phallusia sp.*)
Phallusia are solitary ascidians with an exhalant syphon which is almost as large as the inhalant syphon.

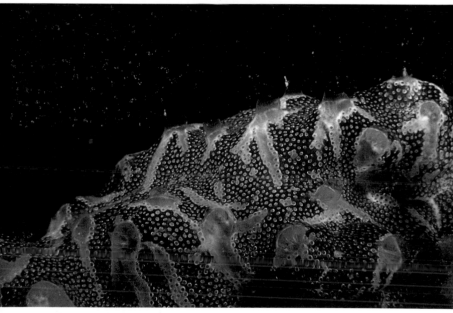

Botrylloides sp.
Botrylloides is a colonial tunicate which forms a fleshy encrusting formation. Individual organisms are arranged around star-shaped crevices in which there is a common exhalant opening.

Clavelina sp.
Clavelina form colonies of delicate transparent individuals approximately 2 cm in height. Their internal organs are detectable from the opaque formations inside the transparent exterior.

Colonial Tunicate
A colonial tunicate with prominent tubular individuals.

Didemnid Ascidian
This didemnid or green grape ascidian takes on an extraterrestrial appearance when viewed in a close-up encounter.

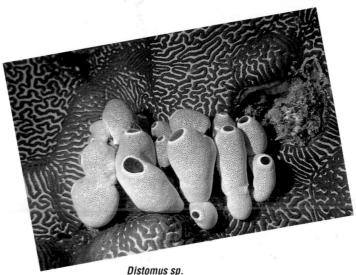

Distomus sp.
Distomus is a colonial tunicate commonly found in the Indo-Pacific. Each individual is about 3 cm in length and is joined at the base by a network of stolons. The body is grey to transparent and the inhalant syphon is ringed with yellow.

Salp
Members of the genus *Pegea* belong to the family Salpidae, commonly known as salps. They are small, pelagic, solitary tunicates that are often transparent in appearance. Their body organs are visible through the transparent body walls.

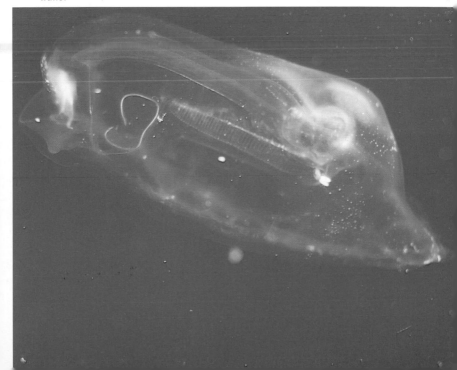

The Formidable Dentition of the Estuarine Crocodile
Although it normally stays close to estuarine waters, the estuarine crocodile is being driven further afield by development and human occupation of its natural habitat. Equally at home in brackish as well as saline waters, the estuarine crocodile could pose a threat to divers if sighted in the vicinity of dive sites.

REPTILES

Divers and snorkellers may encounter members of four major groups of reptiles in the marine environment. They are snakes, turtles, crocodiles and lizards. While marine snakes are no larger than their land relatives, members of the other groups (turtles, crocodiles and lizards) might be considered 'giants' as far as reptiles go.

Sea Snakes

The majority of species of sea snakes inhabiting waters of the South China Sea belong to the family Hydrophiidae. All members of this family are venomous and some are considered deadly. Even though most land snakes are able to swim, the specialised laterally flattened tail of marine snakes is an effective paddle which facilitates movement in water.

The black-and-white banded snake (*Laticauda colubrina*) is one of the most common marine species found in the area. It is marked with alternating bands of black and a pale bluish-grey. The lower jaw and the anterior portion of the underside of the body is tinged with yellow. *Laticauda* is frequently sighted in muddy mangrove swamps and may be seen in Singapore waters around Pulau Sudong.

Little is known about the feeding habits of marine snakes but they are thought to feed on small fish and perhaps molluscs. Unlike most species of sea snakes which are viviparous and remain in the ocean throughout their life cycle, *Laticauda* comes ashore not only to lay its eggs but at other times as well. It may be found out of water, on sandy beaches hiding under rocks or in cracks between large boulders.

Laticauda is not aggressive and will not attack even when provoked. Though unlikely, a bite from *Laticauda* is possible, especially if the snake is stepped on unexpectedly. The bite may seem minor or insignificant at first due to the snake's small jaws and fangs, but

the neurotoxic poison becomes evident after about half an hour, causing stiffening of the muscles and locking of the jaws, and in severe cases, coma and death.

Two other sea snakes common in the area are *Ceberus rynchops* and *Enhydrina schistosa*. *Ceberus rynchops* also inhabits mangrove swamps and is occasionally found on rocky shores and coral reefs. It is a muddy brown or dark grey having black transverse stripes or rows of connected spots. *Enhydrina schistosa* is a uniform grey on the dorsal surface and white underneath. It is smaller than the other two snakes as it reaches only one metre in length.

Banded Sea Snake
(*Laticauda colubrina*)
If it stays around long enough to be observed at close range, the unmistakable markings of *Laticauda colubrina* betray its identify. Its silvery-grey body is evenly banded with about 30-50 black rings. Its flattened tail and relatively small head are black, while the snout tip is yellow. The small head aids in feeding as the snake probes coral crevices for fish eggs and small fish.

Turtles

Most species of marine turtles are much larger than their land relatives. Six species of giant turtles roam the oceans worldwide. Although they are most often found in tropical waters, they sometimes follow warm currents to temperate seas, though they do not remain there for long.

Hawksbill Turtle
(*Eretomochelys imbricata squamata*)
The long snout, beak-like 'overbite' of the upper jaw and the large scales on the head are characteristic of the hawksbill. Hawksbills are carnivorous. By day they rest in caves, coming to the surface to breathe every hour.

Marine turtles, unlike land turtles, cannot retract their heads completely into their shells. They have a compressed streamlined shell and broad, flattened forelimbs. The forelimbs act as propellers to expedite movement, while the smaller hind legs help them to manoeuvre and steer. Turtles live and mate at sea, but during the reproductive season females return to the beach on which they themselves emerged as hatchlings, to lay their eggs. This journey often entails impressive feats of navigation and endurance as they make their way from their customary feeding grounds to a specific beach. It has been estimated that some female turtles travel hundreds, or even thousands of kilometres for the purpose of laying their eggs.

Once the female turtles arrive in waters off the beach of their destination, they wait for adequate cloud cover before approaching the beach. Built for travel in the ocean, giant turtles are slow and clumsy on land, pulling themselves laboriously onto the upper reaches of the beach before selecting a site suitable for laying eggs. Using their hind flippers, the female turtle scoops out flipperfulls of sand to create a deep hole into which up to 90 or 100 eggs are deposited. After the eggs are laid, the hole will be carefully refilled, scoop by scoop, with the same pile of sand that was removed earlier. Finally exhausted, with mucus streaming from her eyes, the female makes her way back to the water and speeds her way out into the ocean.

Though air breathing, turtles are able to spend large amounts of time under water, coming up for air approximately once in three hours. Their preference is for open water, but they can occasionally be found around off-shore reefs or quite close to the shore, even when they are not laying. They apparently visit reefs to take advantage of the feeding opportunities available there.

Because of the nature of their egg-laying habits, many species of marine turtles are endangered. Their eggs are delicious and fetch a good price at local markets. The stretches of Malaysian beaches where turtles lay their eggs are long and often deserted. Despite concerted efforts by the Malaysian government in ensuring the preservation and survival of these remarkable creatures, poaching of turtle eggs is very difficult to control. Government sponsored hatcheries are now responsible for a good number of hatchlings that return to the ocean to sport their chances of reaching adulthood.

The most common turtles found in local waters are the green turtle (*Chelonia mydas japonica*), the hawksbill turtle (*Eretomochelys imbricata squamata*), the loggerhead turtle (*Caretta caretta*), and the leatherback turtle (*Dermochelys coriacea schlegelli*).

Green Turtle
(*Chelonia mydas japonica*)

An occasional visitor to the reef, the green turtle is not green in its outer appearance: its carapace is actually a mottled brown colour. The name 'green' turtle is derived from the colour of the body oil, which gives the greenish colour to the famous green turtle soup. The green turtle can grow up to 1.2 metres in length and 150 kg in weight.

After her egg-laying session, the female green turtle makes her way to more familiar territory. Female turtles may make several visits to a particular stretch of beach during each laying season.

Green turtles have been indiscriminately hunted over many years and rank high among the world's endangered species.

Leatherback Turtle
(*Dermochelys coriacea schlegelli*)

Coming ashore to lay eggs is a demanding task for the female leatherback. Being the world's largest species of turtle, mature female adults can weigh up to 650 kg. The ridged shell or carapace reaches 1.5 metres in length but is not made up of the flat bony plates characteristic of most marine turtles but of many thin, rib-like structures arranged in parallel fashion and covered with a tough, leathery integument.

Female leatherbacks come on shore to spawn three or four times each laying season. Each time they lay 90–150 eggs. Looking like billard balls, the eggs are deposited in a deep narrow hole dug by the hind flippers. The mucous tears shed during the leatherback's time on shore are popularly thought to be a sign of exhaustion, but are more likely to be a means of lubricating the eye. The tears are also very salty and therefore are thought to be a means of excreting excess salt from the body.

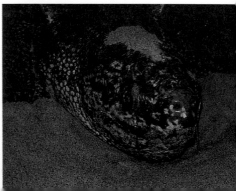

183

Monitor Lizard (*Varanus salvator*)
Although not strictly marine reptiles, monitor lizards are effective swimmers, often migrating to small islands off the mainland. They snatch live fish which swim near to shore or they may live on carrion on the shoreline.

Crocodiles and Lizards

Although crocodiles were a definite hazard to swimmers about 25 years ago, it would be unusual nowadays to find a large crocodile where divers and snorkellers engage in their sport. Nevertheless, it is possible to find a large estuarine crocodile, *Crocodylus porosus*, in estuarine waters. It is also known that estuarine crocodiles migrate from the rivers of Johor into Singapore waters.

Even when encountered at a distance, crocodiles must be regarded as highly dangerous. There are numerous accounts of deliberate attack, particularly on children. In each case, victims are first of all unbalanced by a blow delivered by the crocodile's powerful tail. Thereafter, the crocodile seizes the victim firmly in its jaws and drags it under water thus defeating all attempts by the victim to restore balance and retreat on foot.

In spite of their intimidating and even hostile appearance, estuarine crocodiles are sociable creatures within their own species. They communicate with each other by a variety of high pitched and deep throated noises. They are also highly territorial.

Crocodiles have been hunted for generations for their skins and this has helped to keep the population down. Similarly, extensive coastal development has tended to disrupt their estuarine habitat and diminish their numbers.

As for lizards (which are close relatives of the crocodile), the monitor lizard, *Varanus salvator*, is a common land dweller in natural jungle as well as jungle reserves and many are found roaming offshore islands. Being a good swimmer, the monitor lizard will retreat to rivers and lakes as a protective measure. Considering the fact that they are not aquatic animals per se, they can remain under water for considerable periods of time. They will sometimes venture into the sea and migrate to small offshore islands where they feed on eggs, crabs and small birds. They also forage for carrion on the littered shore.

Large specimens of monitor lizards reach an impressive size of two metres. They tend to be evasive, however, and to disappear rapidly when humans invade their territory. In an accidental encounter, the monitor lizard will deliver a lash from its huge muscular tail to remind the intruder to treat it with respect.

DOLPHINS

Dolphins are members of the order Cetacea to which whales and porpoises also belong. All Cetaceans are aquatic mammals. They are warm blooded, have an advanced brain and sensory organs, and they give birth to well-developed young. Females nourish their young with milk formed in mammary glands and the mother-young relationships of dolphins are reported to persist over several years.

The most common dolphins found regionally are commonly known as 'bottle-nosed' dolphins and have the scientific name: *Dolphinus delphis*. The spindle-shaped body of bottle nosed dolphins reaches 2 metres in length and is propelled with a powerful tail. Their dorsal surface is blackish-brown, having a sail-shaped dorsal fin about halfway along the body. The ventral surface is a paler grey. As their common name suggests, the nose of bottle-nosed dolphins is elongated. The upper jaw is beak-shaped and protrudes a little beyond the lower jaw. Both jaws bear prominent teeth, which are advantageous in catching the fast-moving squid and fish that comprise the dolphin's diet.

Dolphins are seen in all locations in the South China Sea. They sometimes venture as close to shore as dive sites, but more often they are sighted in stretches of water between islands. Occasionally, schools of dolphins accompany the boat over some distance, riding the crest of the wave created by the dipping bow.

Dolphins are graceful, gregarious and playful creatures. They appear to take great delight in leaping out of the water in what seems like a great expression of joyfulness. Dolphins are also noted for their friendliness to human beings. This is true not only for captive individuals, but also for those that are in their natural habitat. Even so, nowadays, schools of dolphins have become highly cautious and seem to do a 'disappearing act' when divers enter the water!

Apart from becoming a major source of entertainment at marine parks, dolphins have also become subjects of scientific interest due to their apparent intelligence and ability to communicate with their own kind. They have a remarkable hearing ability. Tests on bottle-nosed dolphins show that they not only hear through the human range, but their hearing capacity reaches ten times the upper limit of humans (to about 150 kilohertz)!

Dolphin (*Dolphinus delphis*)
Dolphins are as playful in their natural environment as they are in captivity. They enjoy riding the crest of the waves created by the dipping bow of a boat. Sometimes a school of dolphins will divert into a bay to frolic, taking their turn to leap out of the water in graceful somersaults.

Remora on Leopard Shark
Apart from getting a free ride wherever they go, remoras scavenge morsels of food left behind by the shark's kill. They are also believed to feed on parasites on their host shark's skin.

SPECIAL RELATIONSHIPS

While all organisms that exist within a reef ecosystem are to a certain degree interdependent, some interesting and highly specialised forms of interdependent relationships can be found among coral reef inhabitants.

Terms that are commonly used to describe different types of association and interdependence among living organisms are: symbiosis, commensalism, mutualism, and parasitism.

Whenever an interdependent relationship exists between two organisms, this may be described as a symbiotic relationship. If one of the two organisms benefits significantly more than the other, and the host is not affected much, then the relationship may be referred to as commensalism. If both organisms benefit, then the relationship can be called mutualism. If one of the symbionts benefits at the expense of the host organism (to the extent that the host may ultimately die) then the association is referred to as parasitic.

Most special relationships illustrated in this section of the guide are commensal relationships. The term commensal actually means to 'eat at the same table'. Although eating 'at the same table' should be loosely applied here, the types of symbiotic relationships that exist on a typical reef have a lot to do with obtaining food as well as securing camouflage and protection.

Anemone on Hermit Crab

Hermit crabs are scavengers commonly seen along the shoreline. Although they have typical features of a crab, the coiled soft abdomen is more vulnerable than that of most of their relatives.

Hermit crabs lack the protection of a hard exoskeleton. The diminished hind end of the hermit conveniently fits into the internal cavity of an empty snail shell.

Anemone on Hermit Crab
These anemones seem to experience no adverse effects arising from a peripatetic existence. On the contrary, they are at a vantage point to obtain scraps of food rejected by their hermit crab host.

Since the shells inhabited by hermit crabs are not simultaneously occupied by a living mollusc, the typical hermit crabs' life-style cannot be described as a commensal relationship. However, certain species of hermit crabs seek another type of association by covering their shells with sea anemones. Being venomous, the anemones ensure that potential predators avoid the crab. The precarious mobility offered to the anemones does not seem to affect them adversely at all. They open up and retract their tentacles when feeding, much as they would if their habitat was a fixed substrate.

The anemones are at a vantage point to obtain scraps of food that are released by the crab as it is feeding. However, there is one report of a hermit crab deliberately extending its hospitality to the anemones on its shell. This particular crab was kept in an aquarium and was receiving a meal of dead fish. Apparently, after eating its share of the fish, the crab was seen to reach up and offer some to the anemones on its shell!

When the hermit crab retreats into its shell, the front pincers carefully complete the protection by sealing off the shell's entrance. When the hermit crab needs to move around to feed, it protrudes its head and legs from the aperture of the shell and moves at an impressive pace!

Sharks and Their Attendants

Several species of fish commonly associate themselves with sharks and are often seen travelling with them. These fish have varying degrees of dependency on the shark. For instance, jacks surf on the bow wave in front of the shark while pilotfish swim freely alongside them. Contrary to common belief, pilotfish do not lead the shark to its prey (as might be inferred from their name). Both the jacks and the pilotfish are loosely associated with the shark and derive benefit from staying close to it. They are able to share morsels of food from the shark's kill and they are unlikely to be attacked by predators as long as they stay close to the shark.

Remora on Shark
Remoras or suckerfish are frequently associated with sharks. The special sucker pad on the top of the head is a highly modified dorsal fin. This pad acts as a vacuum suction pad enabling the remora to hold on to the shark.

Remoras or shark suckerfish gain similar benefits but associate themselves closely with sharks as well as other large fish. They actually attach themselves by means of a specialised suction pad located on the top of their heads. They are also thought to be of some benefit to the shark by removing parasites from the shark's body. Occasionally, it becomes evident that sharks would like to rid themselves of their remora passengers. It is not unusual to see the reef white-tip shark rolling on the sea bed in an apparent attempt to dislodge an annoying remora.

Cleaner Wrasse (*Labroides dimidiatus*)

The cleaner wrasses are small specialised fish with long pointed snouts and tweezer-like jaws. Their distinct form and striped body distinguishes them as cleaner fish rather than prey. This inhibits attack.

Cleaner wrasse usually live in pairs adjacent to caves or near prominent coral boulders. Their 'cleaning stations' can easily be identified by fish seeking their cleaning service. The stations are even frequented by larger fish such as morays and groupers. Larger fish may open their extensive jaws and gill covers while cleaner fish scavenge inside their mouths.

Cleaner wrasse are absolutely essential to the health of other fish on the reef. A reduction in the population of cleaner wrasses will lead to a decline in the health of the fish population. It is believed that an absence of cleaner fish altogether leads to the virtual abandoning of the reef by the rest of the fish population.

Blue-streak Cleaner Wrasse (*Labroides dimidiatus*) with Surgeonfish
Essential inhabitants of every reef, cleaner wrasse act like reef medics removing bacteria and other parasites from the skins of much larger fish. Measuring about 8 cm in length, the blue-streak cleaner wrasse is a very common sight on most reefs. Juvenile forms of this species are black with a blue stripe.

Cleaner Wrasse with Moray
This moray is enjoying the attention of not one, but two cleaner wrasse. More daring cleaner fish may, on occasions, venture into the moray's mouth!

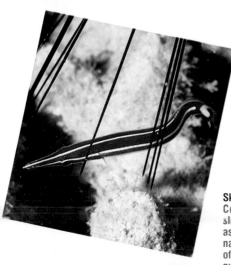

Pipefish in Sea Urchin
The dangerous spines of the sea urchin provide a safe haven for this daring, well-camouflaged pipefish. They are virtually undetectable when they position themselves parallel to the sea urchin's spines.

Skunk Shrimp
Commonly found in pairs, skunk shrimps perform much the same task as cleaner fish. They are indiscriminate 'pickers' and have a wide range of willing clients. Skunk shrimps frequent moray eel hideouts.

Periclimenes Shrimp

Some crustaceans avoid detection by potential predators by developing relationships with other invertebrates such as sea anemones, molluscs (usually nudibranchs) and echinoderms. One of the most successful groups in engaging in this type of relationship are the numerous species of shrimp belonging to the genus *Periclimenes*.

The body of some species of *Periclimenes* are so transparent that they are barely visible against their host. In fact, their interspersed, solid white markings make them look more like dismembered corpses than living animals.

Other species of *Periclimenes* acquire effective camouflage by being the same colour and having similar markings to their host. One excellent example of such camouflage is the species that associates itself with the large nudibranch: *Hexabranchus*.

While the nudibranch is resting, the shrimps are concealed in a fold of the mantle or under the branches of the gills. As the nudibranch moves around, the numerous folds and undulations of its body allow the shrimp to dart around undetected. It is believed that *Periclimenes* will stay with its original host for life although the benefit for the host in having such timid guests is unclear.

Periclimenes on _Hexabranchus_
Members of the genus *Periclimenes* have developed an association with other invertebrates such as anemones, nudibranchs and sea cucumbers. These organisms have developed very effective camouflage that mimics the colour and markings of their host.

Periclimenes on Sea Cucumber

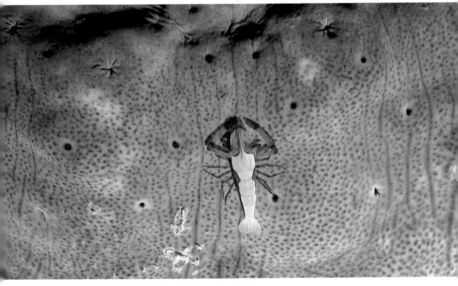

Crab in Crinoid
This tiny spider crab is camouflaged among the protective arms of the feather star. The precise relationship between these two organisms is not fully understood.

Anemonefish (*Amphiprion sp.*)

Anemonefish are sometimes called clownfish because their markings resemble the painted face and striped attire of a clown. Their antics as they dodge in and around the tentacles of their anemone host might also be described as clown-like.

There are many species of anemonefish found in the South China Sea. More common species are the striped anemonefish, the pink or skunk anemonefish and the African black anemonefish.

Each species of anemonefish favours a particular anemone host and there is much debate as to the respective benefits of the anemonefish anemone relationship. Certainly, anemonefish attack coral-eating fish which come too close to their host. They also eat parasites affecting the anemone. In turn, anemones sting fish which might attack the anemonefish. But anemonefish are never seen living separately from the anemone whereas the reverse is true, without any apparent ill-effects.

The black anemonefish is the most aggressive of the three species. When it is young it will tolerate others of its species. As it grows older, however, it will tolerate only its mate with which it appears to form a permanent partnership. The eggs are laid among the tentacles of the anemone and they are guarded by both male and female during the development period. Others lay their eggs on bare rocks next to the anemone and guard them until they hatch.

How do anemonefish avoid getting stung by the anemone? They do it simply by coating themselves with a mucous covering from the anemone itself. First of all they rub against the underside where there are no tentacles. They continually maintain this mucous coating as they move among the tentacles. It is believed that a chemical in the mucous prevents the release of the stinging cells in the tentacles of the anemone.

Anemonefish (*Amphiprion sp.*)
Anemonefish are often referred to as 'clownfish'. But in fact, only one species of anemonefish justifies the name 'clownfish'. Anemonefish are well-known for their association with sea anemones. The stinging nematocysts on the tentacles of the anemone host do not adversely affect the anemonefish because of the mucous coating it acquires while rubbing itself against its host. Not only do they seek protection within the folds of the anemone, they also take advantage of scraps of food derived from the anemone's prey.

Clown Anemonefish
(*Amphiprion ocellaris*)

The slender body of this anemonefish is bright orange with three distinct vertical white bands. All the fins are orange outlined in black. The clown anemonefish feeds on zooplankton and seaweed.

Red and Black Anemonefish (*Amphiprion melanopus*)
In the adult form, *Amphirion melanopus* is bright orange with a single white bar over the head. The hind region of the body as well as the pelvic and anal fins, are usually marked with black. There are definite regional differences however and colouration is also purportedly linked with the species of anemone host with which the individual associates.

Clark's Anemonefish
(*Amphiprion clarkii*)

This species exhibits great colour variation. The body ranges frrom bright orange to black while the tail may be white, yellow or black. Often an adult pair and some juveniles will be found in one anemone host.

Stonefish (*Synanceia horrida*)

The formidable and hideous-looking stonefish grows to a length of 30 cm. Its 'bottom-heavy' physique is suited to its life as a sedentary, bottom dweller. Its appearance convincingly resembles a piece of coral or rock.

The stonefish will not deliberately attack human intruders, but it is highly dangerous if inadvertently trodden upon. What makes the stonefish particularly dangerous is the fact that it is so difficult to detect. It remains buried in the ground most of the time with only the stalked eyes and mouth protruding above the surface of the sand. Even when it is perched on rocks, poised on its pectoral fins, it is camouflaged by algae and other organisms that encrust its warty skin.

Stonefish can change their entire skin when they need to alter their camouflage. This is done by dramatic swelling movements followed by rapid deflation of the body. This causes the old outer layer of the skin to peel off so that a new one is revealed.

The stonefish feeds on living prey, but uses its poison spines as a means of defence (rather than as a means of attack). Passing prey will be instantly sucked into the doortrap mouth and swallowed whole. The dorsal fin carries 13 sheathed spines that normally lie flat against the body. Contained in each spine is a poison gland that contains lethal venom. If the spines come into contact with an intruder, they pierce the skin delivering the venom through grooves in the spines.

Immediate intense pain which increases over the ensuing 10 minutes, may cause the victim to faint. This reaction may be followed by fever, sweating and pallor. Numbness and paralysis may later affect adjacent muscle tissue. Delirium and mild respiratory failure as well as cardiovascular collapse is not uncommon. Death may occur in extreme cases.

Stonefish
(*Synanceia horrida*)
Formidable is their appearance and formidable the venomous potential of the stonefish. The 13 spines on the dorsal fin are virulently venomous. Two of these spines can be seen on this specimen on the anterior portion of the dorsal fin, just behind the eyes. The pectoral fins are fleshy and often extended when the fish remains in its motionless state.

False Stonefish
Also called a toadfish, the false stonefish has a smoother skin and is less pitted in appearance when compared with the true stonefish. The eyes of the false stonefish are curiously placed in the centre of protruding spheres.

Scorpionfish (*Scorpaenopsis sp.*)
The colour of scorpionfish varies according to their habitat. The organisms that colonise the scorpionfish's warty skin provide camouflage, making it virtually undetectable when ensconced among rocks and coral rubble.

Scorpionfish (*Scorpaenopsis sp.*)

Scorpionfish belong to the family Scorpaenidae and many members of this genus somewhat resemble stonefish in appearance and habits. They inhabit rocky reefs and are often found in moderately deep to shallow water. Their warty skin is frequently covered by algae and other organisms which combine to form a remarkable camouflage. Like the stonefish, they remain immobile for long periods of time with their pectoral fins extended. They are so well camouflaged that they resemble a rock or piece of coral.

Apart from their grotesque appearance, scorpionsfish can be distinguished by the numerous fleshy, weed-like growths that protrude from their lower jaws, snout and body. Their dorsal fin contains several (up to 12) sheathed, venomous spines which release venom when they penetrate the victim's flesh. The effect on the victim will be similar to but less severe than the effect of stonefish.

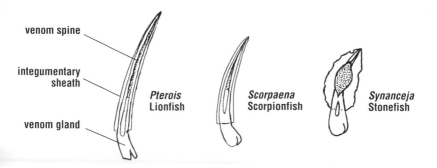

venom spine

integumentary sheath

venom gland

Pterois
Lionfish

Scorpaena
Scorpionfish

Synanceja
Stonefish

Lionfish (*Pterois sp.*)
This is another impressive profile of a different species of lionfish with shorter flaps above the
eyes. This particular species
also has protrusions dangling
from the lower jaw.

Lionfish (*Pterois sp.*)

Presenting one of the most magnificent sights on the reef, the
lionfish offers a fine display with its long plume-like dorsal and pectoral fins.

These fins wave languidly when the fish is at rest, but spread omi-
nously when it is disturbed. But the plume-like fins have an ominous
rather than ornamental function! Along their length lie a series of
formidable poison glands. Although they do not launch a direct
attack unless deliberately provoked, lionfish should be viewed at a
distance, as wounds inflicted by their fins can be very painful.

Lionfish are rarely seen out in the open during the day, but they
can be seen in caves or on ledges, sometimes in an upside down position. They are often seen in groups of three or more.

Lionfish (*Pterois sp.*)
The long tessellated flaps above the
eyes of this species of lionfish resemble horns. Their precise function is
unknown but they are believed to be
sensory. Fine hair-like flaps are visible
above the nostrills in this specimen.

Zebra Lionfish (*Dendrochirus zebra*)

The zebra lionfish looks threatening with its fins extended. But, like other lionfish, it uses its venomous spines more as a means of defence than as a means of attack. This species is distinguishable by the continuous fin membranes on the pectoral fins and the long protrusions located on the upper surface of the eyes. Reaching up to 30 cm in length, the zebra lionfish is large compared to other lionfish.

Longhorn Lionfish (*Pterois radiata*)

The spines of the dorsal and pectoral fins of the longhorn lionfish are long and intensely white. Another distinctive feature of this species is the long and delicate protrusions above the eyes.

Plumed Lionfish (*Pterois volitans*)

Also called a turkeyfish, this species of lionfish has long, falcated (plume-like) dorsal and pectoral fins. When they are spread out, the pectoral fins appear much like wings. These wing-like pectoral fins are effective in cornering prey in coral crevices. Once the prey is cornered, the lionfish will lunge forward and gulp down its prey in less than a split second.

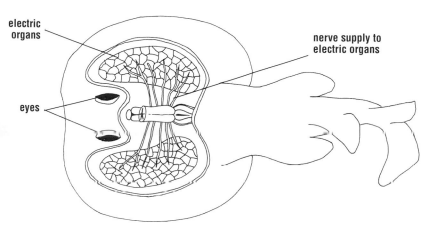

electric organs

nerve supply to electric organs

eyes

Electric Ray (*Hypnos sp.*)

The electric ray is sometimes called a torpedo ray, even though they are slow, ineffective swimmers. Their usual habit is to lie submerged in sand or mud. The electric ray can deliver a strong electric shock which is generated by the electric organs.

The electrical discharge varies from 8 to 220 volts and passes between the negative, ventral side and the positive, dorsal side of the ray. The electrical discharge is actually a successive series of discharges stimulated by tactile sensations. The electric shock is sufficient to disable an adult and may have an even more serious effect on a child. Drowning may result from the drastic effect of the electric shock.

Electric Ray (*Hypnos sp.*)
If accidentally touched, the electric ray can give off an electrical discharge that will give the intruder a severe electric shock.

Blue-spotted Lagoon Ray (*Taeniura lymma*)
In a characteristic retreat, this blue-spotted lagoon ray is heading for a protective ledge. Divers should beware of the pair of venomous spines at the base of the whip-like tail.

Blue-spotted Lagoon Ray (*Taeniura lymma*)

The blue-spotted lagoon ray is a timid creature that usually buries itself in the sand and retreats at the slightest advance of a diver. However, it possesses a pair of venomous spines in the base of the tail and, if trodden on, the sting can be painful and troublesome.

In order to effect its sting, the stingray lashes its tail upward and forward, driving the spine into the limb or body of the victim. The serrated spine is normally covered by a sheath or integument. When the tail is lashed and the spine released, it can penetrate its target so effectively that it can break off and remain in the wound together with its sheath.

Pain is immediate and severe. The pain increases over 1-2 hours and subsides after 6-10 hours. Nausea, vomiting and diarrhoea may also result. The poison tends to affect the lymphatic glands, so muscular cramps can be experienced in adjacent muscle tissue.

Textile Cone (*Conus textile*)

Because of their attractive colouration and exquisite markings, cone shells are a favourite of shell collectors. They may reach a length of 10 cm and are found in shallow waters often buried in the sand. What may be immediately visible is the orange-ringed syphon which projects from the sand and takes in water for respiration. The dangerous part of the animal is the proboscis which extends outwards from the narrow end of the shell aperture.

The proboscis is the vehicle through which the cone shell projects its minute harpoon carrying 1-20 radulae or teeth. These teeth are able to penetrate the skin and inject a venom which immobilises the victim. The harpoon is sharp enough to penetrate clothing.

Textile Cone (*Conus textile*)
The modified radula (or harpoon) of the cone shell, which delivers the venom of the organism's sting, is located in the animal's proboscis. The harpoon is usually not visible unless the animal is attacking its prey. The proboscis should not be confused with the syphon which is usually visible as the textile cone moves. The proboscis can also be directed backwards so even careful handling can prove fatal and should be avoided at all costs!

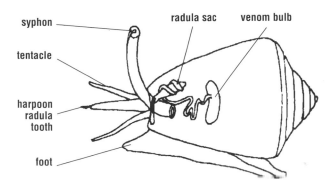

VENOM APPARATUS OF A CONE SHELL

syphon

radula sac   venom bulb

tentacle

harpoon
radula
tooth

foot

Numbness from the sting may extend to the rest of the body. The mouth and lips are especially affected. Muscular paralysis occurs. Speech and visual interference is evident within 10-30 minutes of the sting. Respiratory failure is also possible.

Stinging Hydroid (*Lytocarpus sp.*)

This fern-like hydroid is common in local waters and is often a dull, brownish colour. However, some varieties range from purple to silvery-white.

Contact with *Lytocarpus* ranges from a mild stinging sensation to extreme pain. Pain increases over the first 10 minutes. The skin becomes patchy with pinpoint lesions. The sting results in ulcerial weals in the first 2-4 hours. Blotches turn red and a rash may result from swelling and ulceration of the skin. The affected area becomes swollen and there is discomfort and itching. Pigmentation of the skin may be the eventual result.

Stinging Hydroids
Tiny polyps border the fronds of this delicate hydroid. Hydroids are not light dependant and can be found in many different niches on the reef.

Stinging hydroids (*Aglaophenia sp.*)
Hydroids are often found growing around the opening of caves. This poses a threat to divers who are prone to investigating the interior of caves without due caution!

Stinging Nettles (*Lytocarpus*)
The innocent, feathery-looking sea nettles such as *Lytocarpus* are one of the most common causes of stings to divers. The stings can often result in a rash which can erupt into welts and become a prolonged source of discomfort.

Lion's Mane Jellyfish
The lion's mane jellyfish has exceptionally long tentacles. Larger specimens can have tentacles measuring up to 10 metres in length and their fine tips are both fragile and laden with nematocysts. The tentacles can keep their stinging capability for some time after they have broken off and so a diver coming into contact with the tentacles may be unaware of the source of discomfort.

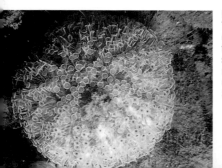

Flower Urchin (*Toxopneustes pileotus*)
The flower urchin is beautiful to look at, but dangerous to touch. The pedicellaria contain small, pink venom sacs. The toxin is sufficently potent to affect the nervous and respiratory systems of the victim. Serious damage to the respiratory system may arrest breathing.

Flower Urchin (*Toxopneustes pileotus*)

The flower urchin is an attractive species of sea urchin with short spines which are barely visible among the enlarged white flower-like pedicellaria. Contact with the spines can cause swelling and discomfort as the tips of the spines often remain in the wound. The immediate area around the injury will become numb and the tip of the spine is virtually impossible to remove.

More severe systemic effects may become evident after a minute and last for more than six hours. There will neurological damage leading to respiratory distress. Breathing may even be arrested as the victim experiences more and more difficulty in inhaling air. In this case, the victim should be immobilised and the appropriate assistance given.

Sea Snake (*Laticauda sp.*)

There are about 50 species of sea snakes in all, but a common type that inhabits waters in the South China Sea is the banded sea snake of the genus *Laticauda*. These snakes reach 1.5 metres in length and feed on live fish. They inhabit shallow coastal waters, breeding and laying their eggs on shore. Banded sea snakes have a laterally flattened body and a flattened paddle-shaped tail. Their greatly enlarged lungs enable them to remain under water for long periods of time.

Bites from banded sea snakes are rare, partly because the mouth and jaws are too small to effect a bite. However, these snakes are equipped with large teeth associated with their poison fangs. Four teeth marks result from the bite; sometimes the teeth stay in the bite. The victim experiences weakness along with paralysis, muscular spasms or twitching. Venom from the bite may also cause tubule damage in the kidneys which inevitably results in death.

Sea Snake (*Laticauda colubrina*)

The venom of banded sea snakes is located in poison sacs at the base of its two pairs of fangs. Injected venom causes weakness, paralysis and/or muscular spasms in the victim. The kidneys of the victim can also be affected.

Diver with Crown-of-Thorns
Crown-of-Thorns is an avaricious feeder favouring staghorn coral for its diet.
In spite of the tough spiny exterior, its body is surprisingly flexible. Here, part
of its body is curled around the coral head on which it is feeding.

Some species of sea cucumbers are large and bulky. Picking them up may cause them to eviscerate, which is their natural defensive mechanism. While growing new internal organs to replace the ones they eviscerated, they are vulnerable to natural predators.

THE REEF'S LATEST INVADERS

Compared to the millions of years it has taken for the world's coral reefs to reach their present stage of development, the hordes of sport diving humans that now invade them are a fairly recent event. With ever more sophisticated self-contained underwater breathing apparatus (SCUBA) or simply with a mask, snorkel and flippers, human beings can now freely explore the wonders of the underwater world and marvel at its living beauty.

Can the reefs of the South China Sea survive this onslaught? With sport diving becoming an increasingly popular pastime of locals and visitors to the region, recreational divers that venture into the reefs unwittingly pose a real threat to the existence of the reef and all the animals that live in and around them.

The biggest threat is posed by collectors who indiscriminately collect anything and everything that looks attractive. But merely the physical presence of divers alone can be destructive. Damage caused by breaking off one piece of coral by a careless flipper can destroy a habitat of hundreds of individual organisms that has taken thousands of years to cultivate.

It is precisely for this reason that the Singapore Club Aquanaut is committed to educating its members on conservation and preservation of coral reefs. The SCA forbids its members to remove any live specimen from the reefs and has set out a strict code of conduct for divers.

While we cannot hope to exert a large influence on the behaviour of the senseless fishermen who blast the reefs, and the commercial enterprises which collect and sell shells for profit, the SCA is intent

A Thoughtless Diver with a Puffer

Blue Linkia (*Linkia multiflora*)
Blue Linkia are among the largest starfish. Picking up and dislodging any organism from its niche can cause it to be disoriented and vulnerable to predators.

upon playing its part in ensuring that sport divers remain innocent of abusing the unique world which they are privileged to enjoy.

We sincerely hope that SCA members and fellow divers will remain sensitive to the fragility of the reef and the balance of life that exists there. Without this concerted effort to observe respect for all living organisms that live in and around the coral reef and without the knowledge necessary to revere it as a unique and specialised marine ecosystem that has taken thousands of years to create, there will be no coral reefs to enjoy in the future.

Diver with sea fan

Juvenile Octopus in a Bottle
Although a Coca-Cola bottle provides a cosy niche for this young octopus, garbage from dive boats thrown into the water by careless divers can create unnecessary damage to the reef environment.

Dead Coral Reef
Nothing is more tragic to a SCUBA diver than to see a reef so utterly devastated by dynamite fishing. Life on this patch of blasted coral will take a long time to return.

CONSERVATION

Once the initial preoccupation with managing SCUBA equipment and buoyancy has been overcome, the sheer joy of being able to move weightlessly underwater is an exhilarating experience in itself. The next step for the SCUBA diver is to take an interest in things outside of himself or herself and to take a peek at what is to be seen in the marine environment.

What there is to see on a dive will depend entirely on the dive location. There are those few hardy souls who enjoy diving in the cold, barren waters of mountain lakes where the water temperatures are enough to wrest the breath out of your lungs. There are even those to whom diving in rivers and drifting with a formidable current provides an incomparable challenge. But for most divers, nothing can compete with the visual impact and the captivating interest of the coral reef, as evidenced by the organisms pictured and described in this book.

Healthy, thriving coral reefs are undoubtedly one of the most exotic and varied natural habitats that exist on earth above or below water. Approximately 600,000 sq km of coral reefs line the coasts of continents and islands as well as dotting the earth's oceans and seas where conditions are most suitable. About 24 per cent of these reefs are located in South East Asia and the highest proportion is situated in the South China Sea.

But sadly, coral reefs in the South China Sea are deteriorating in terms of their overall structure as well as in the growth and population of the reef organisms that inhabit and visit them. Natural forces such as severe wave action resulting from storms and hurricanes, climatic and regional temperature changes, changes in salinity and sedimentation are responsible for some of the damage. But by far the most serious threat to the condition of coral reefs is human intervention of one sort or another.

Littered shorelines such as this one betray a lack of regard for the environment and the life there.

From earliest times, the oceans have been regarded as a useful and abundant provider of food and other items of practical and decorative use. Throughout history, indigenous populations have harvested food from the reefs in quantities that could be replaced naturally. But since deep-freeze technology has been introduced, even into remote places, the quantity of edible organisms now collected is in excess of what can be replaced naturally. Among the

Sedimented rivers such as these deposit the larger particles of silt directly onto the reef and smaller particles remain in the water reducing light conditions and affecting growth of corals.

popular and delectable reef organisms that are on the decline in their natural habitat are octopus (preferred when young), sea cucumbers (considered a delicacy in Chinese cuisine) and seaweed (a favourite of the Japanese). In addition, shellfish such as oysters, clams and scallops, as well as prawn and lobster and even jellyfish are much savoured by gourmets and have assumed a place in one or other of the many Asian cuisines.

Sadly, the reefs that have supported indigenous human populations for generations have in more recent times become grossly exploited by them. Destructive fishing methods such as dynamiting have destroyed many reefs, shattering delicate corals and killing the life that depends on them. Donning SCUBA gear, fishermen position explosives which, when detonated, stun the fish and cause the larger ones to sink to the bottom. These fish can then be collected in a much shorter period of time than by conventional methods. Mild cyanide poisoning is another method used to achieve the same goal.

Now that SCUBA gear has been put to common use by the more enterprising members among indigenous populations, the collection of shellfish for food and decorative use has become a routine, systematic procedure with the effect that many exotic species such as cowries, giant clams and tritons are becoming extremely rare. The prolific shell craft industries which produce anything from hairclips to shoe buckles are testimony to the exploitation of the reef. The sheer numbers of shellfish that have to be sacrificed to make something like a shell curtain, for instance, is mind boggling.

Collection of coral specimens and coralfish for home aquaria is another form of reef plunder that is lucrative and tempting to local fishermen. Unfortunately, a large proportion of the fish that are collected fail to survive the journey to their destination, making their capture a tragic and senseless waste. As soon as the reefs are denuded of one form of life, the entire ecology of the reef is affected. A reef that has been blasted or extensively picked over can take decades to recover, if it ever recovers at all.

Large-scale industrial activities associated with reef areas play no small part in reef destruction either. Dredging for land fills and using fossil reef faces that underlie living corals to make floor tiles and other building materials is highly destructive to marine life. These are excavated at a deplorable rate. Apart from the immediate physical damage, the siltation resulting from this damage is carried by currents to further locations. The same applies to the increased siltation of coastal areas due to deforestation and logging. Silt particles, which originated a long way up river empty into the sea at the river mouth, get carried into the vicinity of the offshore reefs. The particles are either deposited and choke the coral polyps or remain suspended, thus reducing light conditions.

The need to expand the tourist industry to bring in revenue also has its effects. Rapid development of coastal areas and the building of hotels escalates soil erosion which then brings attendant problems of siltation along the coastline. Once a hotel has been built and is occupied, sanitation facilities are often inadequate and disposal of waste is emitted directly into the sea. This results in toxic waste levels which are intolerable to some marine life.

Apart from picking over the reef for much sought-after exotic reef organisms and the large-scale effect caused by development onshore, the sheer number of SCUBA divers in the water has a deleterious effect on reefs. For a start, each time a boat anchors off a coral reef, coral is damaged by the anchor's contact upon entry and removal. Then, careless hands and flippers can break off fragile branches of new coral growth and dislodge delicate reef organisms. The uninformed or ignorant diver will pick up and collect samples of things that look attractive and interesting.

Mention has been made in an earlier section of this book concerning the ways in which divers entertain themselves by provoking pufferfish to puff up to the point that they rise to the surface and

Souvenir shell shops such as this bear witness to the fact that coral reefs are plundered excessively to provide tourists with shell artifacts that will do little else but collect dust.

perish. Other activities which may seem harmless such as grabbing onto turtles and gliding along with them show an equal lack of sensitivity to the organism's right to remain undisturbed. Fish feeding, which is popular in many dive resorts, is also an inappropriate intervention because of the imbalance it creates in the food chain and the unusually aggressive behaviour it evokes in some fish.

Fisherfolk are probably not fully aware of the fact that the devastation they create by using dynamite will affect their long-term livelihood.

Giant turtles in particular are often victims of harassment when they come onto the beach to lay their eggs. They also fall victims to fishing traps and trawling nets. Plastic bags and the kind of balloons that are released in large numbers on festive occasions also pose a threat to turtles that mistake them for jellyfish. The turtles choke to death when trying to swallow their imagined prey.

Clearly, no fisherman intends to destroy his means of livelihood and no SCUBA diver wants to see the end of the natural environment that makes SCUBA such a pleasurable pastime. The thoughtless actions and irresponsible behaviour described above arise more out of ignorance than intent. For one thing, there is the illusion of the fishermen that the reef is indestructible and that it will keep on yielding the desired catch. For another, there is the misconception that removing one tiny organism among so many will not make much difference. The point is that is makes *all the difference*. The organism that is taken could well be the one that has the essential genetic material to enrich the gene pool of the species. It may be that the one that was displaced could have outlasted its many predators to yield yet another generation of the same species.

Assuming that we are conservationist-minded and would like to play a small part in changing the trend towards the deterioration of coral reefs, what can we do?

On first impression it may seem there is little we can do to prevent worldwide exploitation and destruction of coral reefs. However, there is much that we can do by making an impact at a personal level and through conservationist lobbies.

The first thing to do is to become aware of the facts — some of which have been given here. Secondly, we can monitor our own behaviour in the natural environment. We can make the commitment not to disturb any living creature in the reefs we visit. We can keep physical contact with coral reef organisms to a minimum and vouch to *never, ever* collect any species from the ocean. We can encourage others to do likewise and if they are fellow divers, remind them of their responsibilities and insist that any organism they collect must be returned to the water.

Likewise, if we are dealing with a member of the local population who has collected the shell and already killed the organism that once inhabited it, we can refuse to purchase it while politely adding that we would prefer to see the organism alive in the sea. We can resist the temptation to buy any product that has been made with shells, coral or any material derived from what was once a living marine organism.

We can support global efforts to preserve coral reefs and efforts to initiate legislation to protect the reefs and the living forms upon them. The legislation must be such that the collection, distribution and manufacture of objects made with materials from rare and endangered species is unlawful. Steps have been taken in this direction already. CITES (the Convention on International Trade in Endangered Species of Wild Fauna and Flora) has now adopted regulations requiring permits for trade in hard corals in the Order Scleractinia and some soft corals as well.

On another level, there is much that can be done in supporting groups that are engaged in efforts to preserve life on earth and especially on coral reefs, some of which are listed below.

South-East Asia

Malayan Nature Society
PO Box 10750
50724 Kuala Lumpur
Malaysia

**The Nature Society
(Singapore)**
7, Asimont Lane
01–04, Singapore 1130
Singapore

**World Wide Fund for Nature
Malaysia**
Locked Bag 911
Jalan Sultan Post Office
46990 Petaling Jaya
Malaysia

Europe

Marine Conservation Society
9 Gloucester Road
Ross-on-Wye
Herefordshire HR9 5BU
United Kingdom

**Whale and Dolphin
Conservation Society**
19A James Street West
Bath
Avon BA1 2BT
United Kingdom

Earthwatch Europe
Belsyre Court 57
Woodstock Road
Oxford OX2 6HU
United Kingdom

Greenpeace International
Temple House
25 High Street
Lewes
East Sussex BN7 2LU
United Kingdom

Greenpeace International
176 Keizersgracht
1016 DW
Amsterdam
Netherlands

North America

International Oceanographic Foundation
4600 Rickenbacker Causeway
Box 499900
Miami
Florida 33149-9900
USA

Earthwatch Headquarters
680 Mount Auburn Street
PO Box 403
Watertown
Massachusetts 02272-9104
USA

Friends of the Earth
Public Information Office
218 D Street SE
Washington
DC 20003
USA

World Wildlife Fund and the Conservation Foundation
1250 24th Street NW
Washington
DC 20037
USA

National Audubon Society
PO Box 52527
Boulder
Colorado 80321-2527
USA

Center for Marine Education
1725 De Sales Street NW
Washington
DC 20036
USA

Greenpeace, Pacific Campaign
1436 U Street NW
Washington
DC 20009
USA

Australia & New Zealand

Earthwatch Australia
PO Box C360
Clarence Street
Sydney 2000
New South Wales
Australia

Greenpeace, Pacific Campaign
Private Bag
Wellesley Street
Auckland
New Zealand

Local, regional and international groups are active in attempting to prevent further damage to coral reefs. If you become a member you will be better informed to influence others in playing a greater part in conservation. Why not become an active voice in preserving an environment that the earth cannot afford to lose?

adductor muscle: muscle used for pulling together or closing shells of bivalves or barnacles etc.

ahermatypic corals: non-reef-building corals, usually found in deep water; lack zooxanthellae.

Alcyonaria: soft corals; order of Cnidarians.

algae: primitive plants.

Annelids: segmented worms.

Anthozoa: Subphylum which includes hard corals and anemones.

Aristotle's lantern: jaw apparatus in sea urchins consisting of calcareous plates which are moved by a complicated set of muscles.

bivalve: molluscs with two shells eg. clams, oysters.

budding: asexual reproduction where small part of an organism grows out from an individual, eventually developing into another individual (or part of colony).

carapace: hard, bony dorsal covering of Crustacea and turtles.

caudal fin: tail fin.

cephalopods: predatory molluscs eg. squid.

cerata: fleshy finger-like projections on back surface of some nudibranchs, containing undigested nematocyst stinging cells.

Chordate: animals with backbone including vertebrates and urochordates.

cilia: microscopic hair-like projections of some cells used to produce movement.

cirri: jointed appendages found on base of featherstars; used for walking and grasping onto objects.

chloroplast: part of cell containing a pigment used for photosynthesis.

claspers: found in various animals, male appendages used to hold female to facilitate copulation.

Cnidaria: Phylum which includes corals and their relatives.

cnidocil: trigger-like structure which when touched fires nematocysts of Cnidaria.

Coelenterates: Cnidaria.

commensalism: association of two species from which one benefits whilst the other appears not to gain any benefit, but neither is it harmed.

corallite: the cup-shaped structure secreted by a coral polyp.

Crustacea: Phylum of jointed-legged animals.

detritus: particles, often of organic origin, which float in water or settle on sea floor.

diurnal: active during the day.

dorsal: upper (back) surface of animals.

Echinoderms: spiny-skinned radially symmetrical animals with five sections, eg. sea urchins and sea stars.

ecosystem: entire system of organisms living together, interacting with their physical environment.

Elasmobranchs: group of fish with a cartilaginous skelton.

food chain: energy passing from producers to consumers in an ecosystem.

foot: fleshy appendage of molluscs, used for movement.

gastropod: class of molluscs which include snails and nudibranchs.

Gorgonian: Sea fans.

hermatypic: reef-building corals, the cells of which contain zooxanthellae.

Hydrozoa: Class of Cnidarians to which jellyfish and stinging hydroids belong.

lateral: sides of an animal.

mantle: layer of tissue which secretes the shell in most molluscs.

manubrium: protrusion extending from under surface of jellyfish. The jellyfish's mouth is at the end of the manubrium.

massive: dense, non-branched coral form eg. brain coral.

Millepora: fire corals.

Mollusca: Phylum of soft-bodied animals, including gastropods, bivalves, cephalopods.

mutualism: relationship between different organisms where both benefit, often entirely dependent on each other.

nemotocyst: specialised stinging cell containing toxins, found in Cnidarians.

nudibranch: marine slug (literal translation: 'naked gills').

oscellus: marking in fish that looks like an eye ('false eye').

operculum: cover or flap found in many marine animals.

oscula: large exhalant openings in sponges.

parasitism: relationship where one organism benefits to detriment of the other.

pelagic: found living in open waters.

pedicellaria: calcarious pincer-like appendages found on some echinoderms.

photosynthesis: process by which plants use sun's energy to make their own food.

Phylum: broad group of organisms with common characteristics.

phytoplankton: portion of plankton which consists of plants.

plankton: floating organisms, both plants and animals, which are carried along by water movement rather than swimming.

planula: planktonic larval stage of certain marine organisms.

platyhelminthes: flatworms.

Polychaeta: Class of annelids, such as bristleworms.

polyp: sac-like, soft-bodied animal with tentacles round its mouth, characteristic of Phylum Cnidaria.

Porifera: sponges.

proboscis: fleshy, tubular appendage bearing mouthpiece of gastropods.

radiole: feathery structures of certain tube worms used for feeding and respiration.

radula: specialised tooth found in gastropods.

rhinopore: paired, finger-like sensory receptors in most nudibranchs.

rostrum: prolongation of carapace beyond the head in certain Crustaceans.

sabellid: fan worms.

Scyphozoa: jellyfish.

septa: radial plates present in corallites.

Serpulidae: worms secreting calcareous tube.

sessile: attached, not moving

spicules: calcarious, needle-like structures which provide structural support in some invertebrates.

symbiosis: special interdependent relationship between two different organisms.

swim bladder: gas-filled sac which aids buoyancy control.

telson: caudal end of higher Crustacea, which contains anal opening.

tube feet: tiny, extensible hydraulically controlled appendages with suckers at their tips, exclusive to Phylum Echinodermata.

Tunicates: sea squirts.

Urochordata: tunicates.

uropod: last pair of abdominal appendages, found in higher Crustacea, which are flattened and make up tail fin, together with the telson.

ventral: underside of animals.

viviperous: bearing live young.

zooplankton: part of plankton containing free-floating animals.

zooxanthellae: single-celled, photosynthetic algae living in symbiotic manner in tissues of some corals, giant clams, and sea anemones.

Art & Photo Credits

A

Alcyonarians, 30
Algae, 50-53
  Brown, 52
  Green, 52
  Halimeda sp., 52
  Padina sp., 53
  Pink coralline, 50-51
Anemone, Sea, 38-40, 188-189
  Banded tube *(Pachycerianthus maua)*, 41
  Blobbed *(Gyrostoma sp.)*, 40
  Common *(Radianthus sp.)*, 39
  Giant *(Stoichactis sp.)*, 38-39
  Pimply *(Actinodiscus sp.)*, 40
Anemonefish *(Amphiprion sp.)*, 193-194
  Clark's *(Amphiprion clarkii)*, 194
  Clown *(Amphiprion ocellaris)*, 194
  Red & black *(Amphiprion melanopus)*, 194
Angelfish, 92-97
  Blue-ring *(Pomacanthus annularis)*, 95
  Emperor *(Pomacanthus imperator)*, 94
  Mesoleucus *(Chaetodontoplus mesoleucus)*, 92
  Regal *(Pygoplytes diacanthus)*, 93
  Semicircle *(Pomacanthus semicirculatus)*, 96
  Semicircle, juvenile, 96
  Six-banded *(Euxiphipops sextriatus)*, 92-93
  Three spot *(Holocanthus trimaculatus)*, 97
  Yellow-faced *(Euxiphipops xanthometapon)*, 94-95
Annelids, 118, 126-128
Anthozoa, 21
Aristotle's Lantern, 162
Ascidian, 174-176

B

Bananafish *(Caesio pisang)*, 115
Banded Coral Shrimp *(Stenopus hispidus)*, 130
Bannerfish *(see Pennant Coralfish)*
Barnacles, Goose-necked, 129-130
Barracuda *(Sphyraena sp.)*, 76
Basketstar *(Astroboa sp.)*, 161
Batfish *(Platax sp.)*, 4, 102-103
  Pinnate *(Platax pinnatus)*, 103
  Pinnate juvenile, 103
  Teira *(Platax teira)*, 102
Bivalve, Internal stucture, 146
Bivalves, 146

Blue-spotted Lagoon Ray *(Taeniura lymma)*, 69-70, 200
Bony Reef Fish, 72-81
Bottom Dwellers, 106-107
Boxfish *(Ostracion sp.)*, 90
Box jellyfish *(Cubomedusae sp.)*, 21
Bristleworms, 128
Brittlestars, 160-161
  Green-banded *(Ophiarachnella gorgonia)*, 160
  Black-banded *(Ophideris superba)*, 154
  Hairy, 161
Bryozoan, Lacy Sea Mat, 153
Budding, of Corals, 22
Butterflyfish, 104-105
  Bantayan *(Chaetodon adiergastos)*, 105
  Baronessa *(Chaetodon baronessa)*, 105
  Copperband *(Chelmon rostratus)*, 104
  Eight-banded *(Chaetodon octofasciatus)*, 105
  Meyer's *(Chaetodon meyeri)*, 104

C

Camel shrimp, 131
Caridean Prawn, 131
Catfish, Striped, 115
Christmas-Tree Worm, 126
Cave Dwellers, 108-109
Cephalopods, 149-152
CITES, 214
Clams, Giant *(Tridacna sp.)*, 146-147
Classification, of Marine Animals, 17
Cleanerfish *(see Cleaner Wrasse)*
Cleaner Wrasse, 190
Clownfish *(see Anemonefish)*
Cnidarians, 20-49
Cod, Rock *(see Grouper)*
Colouration, of Fish, 56
Commensalism, 188-189
Cone Shell, Venom Apparatus, 201
Cone, Textile *(Conus textile)*, 200
Conservation, Coral Reef, 210
Corals, 20-35
  Ahermatypic, 12
  Anchor *(Euphyllia sp.)*, 27
  Boulder *(Goniastrea)*, 25
  Boulder *(Porites sp.)*, 25
  Bubble *(Plerogyra sp.)*, 26
  Brain, 26
  Cave *(Tubastrea aurea)*, 28
  Daisy boulder *(Goniopora sp.)*, 25
  Dead Man's Fingers *(Sinularia sp.)*, 32

Dendronephthyta sp., 31
Elephant's ear (Sarcophyton sp.), 31
Encrusting, 27
Favia sp., 18-19
Hermatypic, 12
Mushroom (Fungia sp.), 23
Octocoral, 30-33
Plate (Turbinaria sp.), 26
Pumping (Xenia sp.), 33
Sea Fan, 34
Sea Pen, 35
Sea Whips, 35
Soft, 30-32
Staghorn (Acropora sp.), 24
Tree (Dendrophyllia sp.), 27
Tubastrea (Tubastrea aurea), 28
Coral Trout, 78
Coralfish, Pennant (Heniochus
acuminatus), 112
Corallite, 21
Cowrie, 137-138
Arabian (Cypraea arabica), 138
Chestnut (Cypraea spadicea), 137
Tiger (Cypraea tigris), 137-138
Crab, 133-135
Hermit (Dardanus sp.), 133, 188-189
Spider (Xenocarcinus sp.), 135
Sponge (Dromia sp.), 134
Swimming (Thalamita sp.), 134
Crawfish, 132
Painted, (Panulirus sp.), 132
Spiny, 132
Crinoid, (see Feather Star)
Crocodile (Crocodylus porosus), 178-179, 184
Crown-of-Thorns Starfish (Acanthaster
planci), 155-156
Crustaceans, 118, 129-135
Cushion Star (Culcita nouvaeguineae), 158
Cuttlefish (Sepia sp.), 149-150
Cuttlefish, External features, 150

Damselfish, Electric-blue (Pomacentrus
coeruleus), 114
Deterioration of Reefs, 210
Dolphins, 185
Bottle-nosed (Delphinus delphis), 185
Eagle ray, spotted, 69
Earthwatch, 214-215
Echinoderms, 118, 154-171
Elasmobranchs, 61
Electric Ray (Hypnos sp.), 71, 199
Electric-blue damselfish, 114
Emperor Snapper (Lutjanus sebae), 85

Feather Duster Worm, 127
Feather Stars, 170-171
10 armed (Colometra sp.), 171
banded (Lampometra sp.), 171
red (Himerometra sp.), 171

Fire Corals, 44-45
Fish, body shapes of reef fish, 74-75
Fish, External Features, 73
Fish, Schooling, 112-115
Filefish, 81
Flatworms (Platyhelminths), 124-125
Purple spotted, 124
Pseudoceros bedfordi, 125
Pseudoceros buskii, 125
Pseudocerosis corallophilus, 125
Thysanozoon flavomaculatum, 125
Flower Urchin (Toxopneustes pileolus),
165, 202
Flutemouth, Painted (Aulostomus
chinensis), 91
Food Chain, 16
Fugu, 86
Fusiliersfish (Paracaesio sp.), 114

G - K

Gastropods (see Shellfish), 137-145
Goatfish, Common (Mulloidichthys sp.), 106
Goby, Freckled, 106
Gorgonians, 30, 34-35
Greenpeace, 214-215
Grouper (Epinephalus sp.), 77
Hermit crab, 133, 189
Hexabranchus, 192
Hydroid, stinging, 201-202
Aglaophenia sp., 46
Lytocarpus sp., 46-47
Hydrozoa, 44-49
Invertebrates, 118-171
Jack (Caranx sp.), 72-73, 112
yellowtail (Caranx sp.), 112
Jellyfish, 48-49
Lion's Mane, 49, 202
Portuguese Man-Of-War, 20
Kingfish (Rachycentron sp.), 60

L

Lagoon Ray, Blue spotted, 69-70, 200
Leatherjacket, Scribbled (Aluterus scriptus), 81
Leopard shark, 66, 186-187
Lionfish (Pterois sp.), 197-198
Longhorn (Pterois radiata), 198
Plumed (Pterois volitans), 198
Zebra (Dendrochirus zebra), 198
Lizards, 184
Lizard, Monitor (Varanus salvator), 184
Lizardfish (Synodus sp.), 107
Lobster, 132
Slipper (Syllarides squammosus), 132

M

Malayan Nature Society, 214
Manta Ray (Manta sp.), 61, 68
Millepores, 44
Molluscs, 118, 137-152

Monitor Lizard, 184
Moon snail (*Natica sp.*), 140
Moorish Idol (*Zanclus canescens*), 100
Moray Eel, 110-111, 190
  Gymnothorax sp., 111
  Net (*Gymnothorax reticularis*), 110
Murex (*Chicoreus sp.*), 138
Mussel,
  Horse (*Modiolus sp.*), 148
Mutualism, 188

N, O

Napoleonfish (*see Giant Maori Wrasse*), 84
Nematocysts, 20
Nudibranchs, 141-144
  Aeolid, 143
  Chromodoris coi, 141
  Chromodoris quadricolor, 141
  Green spotted (*Nembrotha kubaryana*), 144
  Jorunna, 142
  Melibe sp., 143
  Phyllidia sp., 143
  Rainbow, 144
Nudibranch, eggs, 143
Octopus, 152, 207
Oysters,
  Fluted (*Pycnodonta hyotis*), 147-148
  Thorny (*Spondylus sp.*), 148

P

Painted Flutemouth (*Aulostoma chinensis*), 91
Parasitism, 188
Parrotfish (*Scarus sp.*), 79-80
  Blue (*Scarus sp.*), 80
  Bump-head (*Scarus sp.*), 80
Pennant Coralfish (*Heniochus acuminatus*), 112
Periclimenes sp., 191-192
Phytoplankton, 13
Pilotfish, 189
Pipefish, 191
Plankton, 13
Platyhelminths, 118, 124-125
Pleurobranchus sp., 145
Polyclads, 124
Polyps, 21
  Budding, 22
  External structure, 21
  Internal structure, 22
Porcupinefish,
  Freckled (*Diodon holacanthus*), 88-89
Porifera, 118, 120-123
Portuguese Man-of-War Jellyfish, 20
Prawn, Caridean, 131
Pufferfish, 86-87
  Guinea fowl (*Arothron meleagris*), 87
  Masked (*Arothron sp.*), 87
  Starry (*Arothron stellatus*), 87
  White spotted (*Arothron hispidus*), 86

R

Rabbitfish, 101
  Fox-face (*Siganus vulpinus*), 101
  Spotted (*Siganus sp.*), 101
Rays, 68-71
  Blue spotted lagoon (*Taeniura lymma*), 69-70, 200
  Electric (*Hypnos sp.*), 71, 199
  Giant sting (*Dasyatis brevicaudata*), 71
  Manta (*Manta sp.*), 68
  Spotted eagle (*Aetobatus narinari*), 69
Razorfish (*Aeliscus strigatus*), 113
Reef Fish, Body Shapes, 74-75
Remora, 186-187, 189-190
Reproduction, Budding of Corals, 22
Reptiles, 180-184

S

Sabellids, 128
Salp, 177
Scallop, Fan-shell (*Atrina sp.*), 148
Schooling Fish, 112-115
Scientific names, 8
Scorpaenidea, venom glands, 197
Scorpionfish (*Scorpaenopsis sp.*), 107, 196
Scribbled Leatherjacket, 81
Sea Anemones, 38-40
Sea Cucumber, 166-169
  Alabaster (*Opheodesoma sp.*), 166
  Black & white (*Bohadaschia graeffei*), 168
  Edible (*Halodeima edulis*), 168
  Grey leathery (*Holothuria sp.*), 169
  Leopardfish (*Bohadashia argus*), 168
  Marbled, 168
  Mottled, 167
  Prickly redfish (*Thelanota ananas*), 169
Sea Cucumber, Internal structure, 167
Sea apple, 169
Sea Fan (*Melithaea sp.*), 34
Sea Hare, 145
  Aplysia sp., 145
Sea Mats, Bryozoa, 153
Sea Nettle (*Lytocarpus sp.*), 46-47
Sea Pen, 35
Sea Snake, 180-181
  Ceberus rynchops, 181
  Enhydrina schistosa, 181
  Banded (*Laticauda colubrina*), 181
Sea Stars (*see Starfish*)
Sea Squirts, 173-177
  Botrylloides sp., 172, 175
  Clavelina sp., 175
  Colonial, 175
  Distomus sp., 177
  Pegea sp., 177
  Phallusia sp., 175
  Green Grape Ascidian (*Didemnum sp.*), 174
  Yellow (*Polycarpa sp.*), 173
Sea Squirts, Larval stage, 174
Sea Urchin, 162-165
  Diadema sp. (albino), 163

Flower (*Toxopneustes pileolus*), 165, 202
Banded Long-Spined (*Echinothrix sp.*), 165
Black Long-Spined (*Diadema setosum*), 163
Red Short-spined, 165
Sea Urchin, General features, 164
Sea Whips, 35
Sergeant Major (*Abudefduf sexfasciatus*), 115
Shark, 61-67
  Black-tip reef (*Carcharhinus melanopterus*), 62-63
  Grey Reef Shark (*Carcharhinus sp.*), 61
  Indo Pacific Nurse (*Nebrius concolor*), 64-65
  Leopard (*Stegostoma fasciatum*), 66, 106-187
  Whale (*Rhinocodon typus*), 58-59, 67
  White-tip reef (*Triaenodon obsesus*), 64
Shark, External features, 62-63
Shellfish (Gastropods), 136-140
  Cone Textile (*Conus textile*), 200
  Cowries, 137-138
  Moon snail (*Natica sp.*), 140
  Murex, 138, 139
  Spider conch (*Lambis lambis*), 140
  Top (*Trochus sp.*), 136
  Venus Comb (*Murex sp.*), 139
  Volute (*Cymbiola nobilis*), 139
Shrimp, 130-131, 191
  Banded Coral (*Stenopus hispidus*), 130
  Camel, 131
  Skunk, 191
Singapore Club Aquanaut, 206
Slipper Lobster (*Scyllarides squammosus*), 132
Snapper, Emperor (*Lutjanus sabae*), 85
Soldierfish, Bigeye (*Myripristis sp.*), 108-109
South China Sea, 10
Spiderconch (*Lambis lambis*), 140
Sponge (*Porifera*), 120-123
  Blue, 122
  Green, 123
  Neptune's Cup, 122
  Organ pipe, 121
Sponge, Generalised structure, 121
Spoonworm, 128
Squid (*Loligo sp.*), 151
Squid, External features, 150
Squirrelfish, 108-109
  Adioryx sp., 108-109
  Long-jawed (*Adioryx spinifer*), 109
Starfish, 154-159
  Blue Linckia (*Linckia laevigata*), 157
  Crown-of-Thorns (*Acanthaster planci*), 155-156
  Common (*Protoreaster nodosus*), 159
  Cushion Star (*Culcita nouvaeguineae*), 158
  Linckia multiflora, 157
  Nodular (*Nidorella armata*), 159
  Peppermint Sea Star (*Fromia monilis*), 156
Starfish, Feeding mechanisms, 155
Starfish, Lateral and external features, 154
Stinging Hydroids, 201
Stinging Nettles (*Lytocarpus sp.*), 201
Stonefish, false, 196
Stonefish (*Synanceia horrida*), 107, 195
Surgeonfish, 98-99

Blue (*Paracanthurus hepatus*), 98
Powder-blue (*Acanthurus leucosternon*), 99
White-cheeked (*Acanthurus glaucopareius*), 98
Sweetlips, Many spotted (*Plectorhyncus chaetodontoides*), 78-81
Symbiosis, 189
Synaptid, 166

T

Tang (*see Surgeonfish*)
Textile Cone (*Conus textile*), 200
Top Shell (*Trochus sp.*), 136
Torpedo Ray (*see Electric Ray*)
Triggerfish, 80-81
  Picasso (*Rhinecanthus aculeatus*), 80
  Pink tailed (*Melichthys vidua*), 81
Trout, Coral (*Cephalopholis miniatus*), 78
Trumpetfish (*see Painted Flutemouth*), 91
Tube Anemone, 41
Tubastrea, 28
Tunicates (*see Sea Squirt*), 118, 173-177
Tunicates, Colonial, 174-177
  Botrylloides sp., 173
  Clavelina sp., 173
  Distomus sp., 177
Turtles, 181-183, 213
  Green (*Chelonia mydas japonica*), 183
  Hawksbill (*Eretomochelys imbricata squamata*), 182
  Leatherback (*Dermochelys coriacea schlegelli*), 183

U, V

Unicornfish, smoothhead (*Naso lituratus*), 99
Venom Glands, 197
Venus Comb (*Murex sp.*), 139
Volute (*Cymbiola nobilis*), 139

W, Y, Z

Worms, Flatworms, 124-125
Worms, Segmented, 126-128
  Bristleworm, 128
  Christmas tree (*Spirobranchus giganteus*), 126
  Delicate sabellid (*Sabella pavonina*), 128
  Feather duster (*Sabellastarte indica*), 127
  White sabellid (*Sabella sp.*), 128
Wrasses, 82-85
  Bird (*Gomphosus varius*), 82-83
  Cleaner (*Labroides dimidiatus*), 190
  Giant Maori (*Cheilinus sp.*), 84
  Lyretail (*Thalassoma lunare*), 82
  Speckled (*Anampses sp.*), 85
  Thick lipped (*Hemigymnus melapterus*), 84
Yellowtail Jacks, 112
Zooanthidea, 42-43
Zooplankton, 13, 21
Zooxanthellae, 21

INSIGHT
Pocket Guides

Insight Pocket Guides pioneered a new approach to guidebooks, introducing the concept of the authors as "local hosts" who would provide readers with personal recommendations, just as they would give honest advice to a friend who came to stay. They also included a full-size pull-out map.

Now, to cope with the needs of the 21st century, new editions in this growing series are being given a new look to make them more practical to use, and restaurant and hotel listings have been greatly expanded.

Also from Insight Guides...

Insight Guides is the classic series, providing the complete picture with expert and informative text and stunning photography. Each book is an ideal travel planner, a reliable on-the-spot companion – and a superb visual souvenir of a trip. 193 titles.

Insight Maps are designed to complement the guidebooks. They provide full mapping of major destinations, and their laminated finish gives them ease of use and durability. 100 titles.

Insight Compact Guides are handy reference books, modestly priced yet comprehensive. The text, pictures and maps are all cross-referenced, making them ideal books to consult while seeing the sights. 127 titles.

INSIGHT POCKET GUIDE TITLES

Aegean Islands
Algarve
Alsace
Amsterdam
Athens
Atlanta
Bahamas
Baja Peninsula
Bali
Bali Bird Walks
Bangkok
Barbados
Barcelona
Bavaria
Beijing
Berlin
Bermuda
Bhutan
Boston
Brisbane & the
  Gold Coast
British Columbia
Brittany
Brussels
Budapest
California,
  Northern

Canton
Cape Town
Chiang Mai
Chicago
Corfu
Corsica
Costa Blanca
Costa Brava
Costa del Sol
Costa Rica
Crete
Croatia
Denmark
Dubai
Fiji Islands
Florence
Florida
Florida Keys
French Riviera
  (Côte d'Azur)
Gran Canaria
Hawaii
Hong Kong
Hungary
Ibiza
Ireland
Ireland's Southwest

Israel
Istanbul
Jakarta
Jamaica
Kathmandu Bikes
  & Hikes
Kenya
Kraków
Kuala Lumpur
Lisbon
Loire Valley
London
Los Angeles
Macau
Madrid
Malacca
Maldives
Mallorca
Malta
Manila
Melbourne
Mexico City
Miami
Montreal
Morocco
Moscow
Munich

Nepal
New Delhi
New Orleans
New York City
New Zealand
Oslo and Bergen
Paris
Penang
Perth
Phuket
Prague
Provence
Puerto Rico
Quebec
Rhodes
Rome
Sabah
St. Petersburg
San Diego
San Francisco
Sarawak
Sardinia
Scotland
Seville, Cordoba &
  Granada
Seychelles
Sicily

Sikkim
Singapore
Southeast England
Southern Spain
Sri Lanka
Stockholm
Switzerland
Sydney
Tenerife
Thailand
Tibet
Toronto
Tunisia
Turkish Coast
Tuscany
Venice
Vienna
Vietnam
Yogjakarta
Yucatán Peninsula

NOTES

NOTES